10 Steps to Creating an Infographic

Sara Miller McCune founded SAGE Publishing in 1965 to support the dissemination of usable knowledge and educate a global community. SAGE publishes more than 1000 journals and over 800 new books each year, spanning a wide range of subject areas. Our growing selection of library products includes archives, data, case studies and video. SAGE remains majority owned by our founder and after her lifetime will become owned by a charitable trust that secures the company's continued independence.

Los Angeles | London | New Delhi | Singapore | Washington DC | Melbourne

10 Steps to Creating an Infographic

A Practical Guide for Non-Designers

Stephanie B. Wilkerson

Magnolia Consulting

FOR INFORMATION:

2455 Teller Road
Thousand Oaks, California 91320
E-mail: order@sagepub.com

1 Oliver's Yard
55 City Road
London EC1Y 1SP
United Kingdom

Unit No 323-333, Third Floor, F-Block
International Trade Tower Nehru Place
New Delhi – 110 019
India

18 Cross Street #10-10/11/12
China Square Central
Singapore 048423

Printed in the United Kingdom

Library of Congress Cataloging-in-Publication Data:
2023911125

ISBN: 978-1-0718-1730-8

Acquisitions Editor: Helen Salmon

Editorial Assistant: Paloma Phelps

Production Editor: Aparajita Srivastava

Copy Editor: Beth Hammond

Typesetter: diacriTech

Cover Designer: Scott Van Atta

Marketing Manager: Victoria Velasquez

BRIEF CONTENTS

DETAILED CONTENTS

LIST OF BOXES

CHAPTER 6

CHAPTER 7

CHAPTER 8

CHAPTER 9

CHAPTER 10

PREFACE

When I created my first infographic in 2015, I had no idea what I was doing. I searched for resources offering "how to" guidance and criteria for making a "good" infographic. I found books and blogs on infographics intended primarily for graphic designers developing infographics for marketing, publishing, and journalism. I perused websites offering alluring infographic templates and visually masterful infographics, but I didn't find anything that walked me through the steps of developing a high-quality infographic. What I thought would be a fun endeavor, quickly became a daunting creative challenge. I questioned if I was too linear and process-oriented in my thinking. I am an education researcher and program evaluator, not a graphic designer, after all. I didn't have sophisticated illustration publishing software. I had Microsoft PowerPoint and Word. I also didn't have the budget to purchase expensive software or graphics. And I certainly couldn't afford to hire a graphic designer.

So, what did I do? I did what any resource-savvy person would do: I grabbed the proverbial duct tape and began piecing things together. I culled best practices from infographic books, blogs, and websites and examined innumerous infographic examples. I pulled from my 20 years of experience working with data and communicating information to research and program evaluation audiences. Finally, my process-oriented mind came up with the 10 Steps for Creating an Infographic and the accompanying Checklist for Reviewing Infographics, which captures best practices. In this book, I provide the step-by-step guidance I wish I had when I first started developing infographics. Given its origins, the approach to this book is practical and intended for audiences who want a systematic, user-friendly process for developing infographics with a clearly defined purpose and powerful message. The book's "how-to" approach makes infographic creation accessible for anyone who doesn't have a background in graphic design, a budget for a graphic designer, or duct tape. Even if you have access to a graphic designer, this book will help strengthen your capacity to collaborate meaningfully in the infographic development process.

WHO IS THIS BOOK FOR?

While this book is primarily intended for students and professionals in the research and program evaluation fields, it is appropriate for anyone who wants to translate information into a visual format that communicates a powerful message for readers to remember. Infographics are a communication tool for anyone using data to achieve a clear purpose, whether you study or work in the education, health, or business sectors. Regardless of your education background, this book picks up where much of our undergraduate or graduate training leaves off by covering how to communicate information, including data, in effective visual ways.

FIGURE 1 ■ PLANETS Illustrative Infographic

PLANETS

Think Like an Engineer, Explore Like a Space Rover

The Planetary Learning that Advances the Nexus of Engineering, Technology, and Science (PLANETS)[1] project provides out-of-school time (OST) educators with science and engineering curriculum units that engage learners with science and engineering curriculum units that engage learners in collaborative problem solving through an engineering design process to build learners' habits of mind and improve their attitudes towards engineering.

PLANETS Science and Engineering Units: Remote Sensing, Water in Extreme Environments & Space Hazards

" It really started with learners wanting the problem to be solved—and then they started to persist.
                                    - PLANETS Educator "

Learners demonstrated three habits of mind practices through the engineering design process.[2,3]

Persisting through failure
Evaluating what went wrong in a design, and planning for improvement.

Celebrating successes
When a design improvement results in a positive outcome.

Negotiating designs collaboratively
Working together to design a solution to the given engineering challenge.

Building Habits of Mind

Building habits of mind significantly increased learner attitudes and interest in engineering. [4, 5, 6]

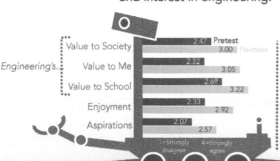

Engineering's:	Pretest	Posttest
Value to Society	2.47	3.00
Value to Me	2.32	3.05
Value to School	2.69	3.22
Enjoyment	2.33	2.92
Aspirations	2.07	2.57

1=Strongly disagree   4=Strongly agree

After PLANETS participation, learners had higher levels of agreement with statements like...

Engineering is useful in helping to solve the problems of everyday life.

We learn about important things when we do engineering in school.

I am interested when we do engineering in school.

Get your learners thinking like an engineer and exploring like a space rover! Access the PLANETS curriculum guides at **planets-stem.org**.

[1] NASA 5-year grant involving a collaborative partnership with the Center for Science Teaching and Learning (CSTL) at Northern Arizona University (NAU), the U.S. Geological Survey (USGS) Astrogeology Science Center, and the Museum of Science, Boston (MOS)
[2] Haden, C. & Peery, E. (2021). Evaluation of the NASA-Funded Planetary Learning that Advances the Nexus of Engineering, Technology, and Science (PLANETS) Project Five-Year Summative Evaluation Report [add link to full report]
[3] The project research and evaluation included 15 out-of-school time settings, 18 out-of-school time educators, and 215 middle school learners.
[4] Lachapelle, C.P. & Brennan, R.T. (2018). An instrument for examining elementary engineering student interests and attitudes. International Journal of Education in Mathematics, Science and Technology (IJEMST), 6(3), 221-240. DOI: 10.18404/ijemst.428171
https://www.ijemst.net/index.php/ijemst/article/view/287
[5] Survey scale sample sizes range n = 150-159. All survey scales are statistically significant at p < .001
[6] Each scale ranged from 0 to 4, with 0 = strongly disagree, 1 = disagree, 2 = not sure, 3 = agree somewhat, and 4 = strongly agree
Mars photo courtesy of NASA/MAVEN/Lunar and Planetary Institute. Milky Way photo courtesy of NASA https://smd-

WHAT SETS THIS BOOK APART?

This book captures important nuances for communicating information and data in the research and evaluation fields and is therefore different than infographic books intended for graphic designers in the marketing, publishing, and journalism fields in the following ways:

- The purpose of infographics in research and program evaluation is to inform an audience, prove a theory of change, or improve a product, practice, or service, not to persuade someone to buy something.

- Researchers and program evaluators strive to maintain methodological credibility through all aspects of a study, including communicating findings. Careful attention must be given to the presentation of positive and negative findings with mindfulness of the potential for bias in selecting what data to include in an infographic.

- Researchers and program evaluators often grapple with condensing large amounts of complex information and data from detailed reports. They confront the challenge of telling an engaging and compelling story that conveys a key message while ensuring results are presented accurately and truthfully.

- Researchers and program evaluators are not graphic designers and will likely not have access to sophisticated design tools and resources, nor do they have the time to learn new software programs. They need guidance on easy-to-use and accessible software programs and resources for creating infographics.

The design of this book breaks down the complex task of developing an infographic through a practical, step-by-step process. Each chapter focuses on learning objectives for one step in the infographic development process and models each step by showing the evolution of an infographic based on an evaluation of the Planetary Learning that Advances the Nexus of Engineering, Technology, and Science (PLANETS) project. This planetary science project was led by the Northern Arizona University Center for Science and Technology with funding from NASA's Science Activation program. Through the PLANETS infographic and other examples presented throughout the book, readers will learn about infographic best practices and tips for applying them during each step in the development process (Figure 1). This illustrative process provides readers with valuable examples of what "to do" and "not-to-do" as well as offers guidance for avoiding design pitfalls. The design challenges in each chapter offer readers an opportunity to apply the steps to learning activities and complex scenarios that might surface during the development process for each step.

FIGURE 2 ■ 10 Steps to Creating an Infographic

10 STEPS

Give data a voice by creating infographics with purpose. Follow these steps to communicate a powerful visual story that your audience will remember.

TO CREATING AN INFOGRAPHIC

10 — REVISE, FINALIZE & SHARE
Revise and refine, based on reviewer feedback. Send for additional review, if needed, and finalize. Disseminate the infographic through social media, email, presentations, and reports.

9 — REVIEW
Select a few people, including audience representatives, to review the infographic using the *Checklist for Reviewing Infographics*.

8 — DRAFT INFOGRAPHIC
Search for templates or create one. Populate your template and ensure that all data displays reflect best practices and that visuals are high quality. Cite credit and copyright information as needed.

7 — SKETCH IDEAS
Sketch various ways you could present the story (consider using a storyboard). Try different ways of displaying the data and other visuals—eliminating anything unnecessary. Refer to the *Checklist for Reviewing Infographics* as an additional guide.

6 — CHOOSE DESIGN ELEMENTS
Choose a color scheme and font types and sizes that promote readability and help organize information. Consider if there is client branding to use. Identify subtle visual cues that will help readers navigate through the story.

5 — SELECT LAYOUT
Decide if you are presenting a hierarchy of information, categories of information, comparisons, a description, or a timeline, and select an appropriate layout. Think about balancing the flow of information on the page to direct focus to the main points. Determine the appropriate size for the infographic for online or print use.

4 — IDENTIFY DATA & VISUALS
Identify visuals that "show" the story. Decide which data are most relevant to the main message. Determine if the visuals and data are culturally-sensitive and sufficient to tell the story, and if you need permission to use them.

3 — CREATE STORY
Create the story's main message, using main points, secondary points, and details that support the infographic's purpose. Determine what foundational information the audience needs in order to understand the main message. Create a call to action or conclusion for the

2 — CLARIFY PURPOSE
Determine what you hope to accomplish through the infographic. Articulate the intended outcome(s) for the audience as a result of reading the infographic.

1 — IDENTIFY AUDIENCE
Identify your audience, their information needs, and their cultural background. Consider how the audience will access the infographic and the context in which they will use the information it contains.

Don't forget to use our *Checklist for Reviewing Infographics!*

For this and other resources, visit magnoliaconsulting.org

magnolia

© 2022 Stephanie B. Wilkerson

WHAT ARE THE 10 STEPS?

The 10 steps are organized into three parts that define the development process: Craft a Powerful Message (Steps 1–3), Design a Visual Story (Steps 4–7), and Bring the Infographic to Life (Steps 8–10). The first three steps help you clarify your audience, purpose, and story for conveying a powerful message through your infographic. The content you create during these three steps lays the foundation for all other design elements. To illustrate, if you're baking a cake, you would first determine who is going to eat the cake and their dietary preferences. Next, you would consider why you are baking it for them—to celebrate or recognize a birthday, anniversary, or special event. Then, you would think about what kind of cake would be most appropriate given the purpose of the occasion and the recipient, and you would find a recipe to follow.

Once you have your content for crafting a powerful message (or recipe for baking a cake), Steps 4–7 walk you through identifying the visual design elements for your infographic including visualizations, layout, colors, and other visual cues for flow. Up to this point, the steps have helped you prepare your ingredients for your infographic "cake." You have determined your cake size and shape, frosting flavor and color, and decorations. You have your equipment and ingredients out on the counter, measured, sifted, sliced, melted, portioned—everything is planned and prepped.

The final Steps, 8–10, involve the mixing, pouring, baking, frosting, and decorating to bring your infographic cake to life. In these steps, you shift from planning to producing. This is where you start building your infographic in your selected software program and make adjustments to your design elements and content through an iterative process, just as you or a "taste tester" might sample the cake batter or frosting and add a little more vanilla extract or flour to get the taste and consistency just right. The final step to the process is figuring out how you want to present your cake—that is, how you are going to get your infographic in front of your audience.

The following describes what you can expect from each step (Figure 2).

Step 1: Identify Your Audience (the "Who")

In the first step, you will learn about identifying the audience for your infographic and think about their information needs and interests. We'll delve into what matters to your audience, how much they understand about your infographic topic, and their level of technical understanding of research and program evaluation.

Step 2: Clarify the Purpose (the "Why")

The second step asks you to clarify what you hope to accomplish through the infographic. I think of this as the intended outcome of your infographic. The purpose of your infographic should align to your audience's information needs. A key question for this step is, "What do you hope will change for your audience as a result of their reading your infographic?" Being exceptionally clear about your infographic's purpose and ensuring subsequent design decisions align to your purpose is key to making your infographic a powerful communication tool.

Step 3: Create the Story (the "What")

The third step in developing an infographic involves defining its central message with main points, secondary points, and supporting details. In effect, you're deciding what story the infographic will tell—that is, what you need to share with your audience to achieve the purpose you defined in the previous step. Your infographic's story is not an afterthought or a by-product of populating a page with attractive images and data visualizations. It is an intentional message you want to convey visually to your audience to create the change you intend.

Step 4: Identify Visuals and Data

In Step 4, you identify the visual elements that will "show" the story you've created. Infographic visuals include icons, photographs, illustrations, data displays, and images. Working from the central message you defined in Step 3, you'll now decide which data are most relevant to the central message and how those data will be presented. In this step, you will determine whether the visuals and data are accurate and sufficient to tell the story. You'll also learn about suggestions for navigating ethical and cultural considerations for communicating information visually.

Step 5: Select a Layout

For Step 5, you will select an infographic format and layout for conveying your key message to your intended audience. You will learn about types of layouts, considerations for layouts based on how you will share it, and how to achieve balance in your infographic's layout. This step also covers different formats of infographics including static, clickable, animated, and interactive.

Step 6: Choose Design Elements

In Step 6, you delve into your infographic's design elements and make decisions about color, font, flow, and focal point. You will learn about online tools and resources for selecting colors and fonts and discover how design elements in an infographic promote readability and help organize information. This step presents tips for using visual cues to help readers navigate through the story.

Step 7: Sketch Your Ideas

In Step 7, you take pencil to paper and sketch various ways to present the story that's emerged in the previous steps. You'll learn different tools and techniques for organizing your ideas and displaying visuals in a clear manner that doesn't detract from your story.

Step 8: Draft the Infographic

All the steps culminate into Step 8 as you bring your design elements together to build your infographic in your selected format and software program. As you move from your sketch to a digital format, this step walks you through the tools, resources, and technical elements you'll use to bring your infographic to life. You'll learn about using online infographic templates or creating your own infographic using Microsoft PowerPoint as well as pros and cons of each. This chapter is the technical, or "how-to," portion of the book. It includes practical tips, online tools and resources, and screenshots of a user creating an infographic using PowerPoint.

Step 9: Review the Infographic

In Step 9, you will learn why the review process is critical to ensuring your infographic accomplishes its intended purpose for your audience. You will learn about considerations for selecting reviewers and how to use the Checklist for Reviewing Infographics to inform the infographic revision process.

Step 10: Revise, Finalize, and Share

In this final step, you will learn about what to expect from the revision process and when you know your infographic is ready for your audience. This step also covers how to disseminate your infographic through social media, embed it in a report, and post it to a website.

WHAT IS MY WISH FOR YOU?

To have fun. Play with ideas. Awaken your inner artist. Don't have one? Then give yourself permission to take creative risks, think outside the box, and try new things. Look for inspiration from other online infographics and visual media. For many of us who work with data and numbers, the creative process might feel overwhelming and outside our comfort zone. This is natural. Learning to communicate information visually might not come easy at first, so be patient with yourself. It will get easier with practice. Remember, you are a consumer of visual information, so think about what you see in visual media that stays with you, makes an impression, and conveys a message you retain.

   While I present the steps in this book sequentially, the process is anything but linear. You will find that you iterate on this process by completing steps, trying ideas, revisiting steps, creating new ideas, and so on. The steps merely ensure your creative process is intentional, thoughtful, and comprehensive. Adjust the process as you need for creative flow. My intention is to bring structure, not rigidity, to creating infographics. As with any recipe, you can follow the steps closely or modify for your personal taste. The development process may not be a piece of cake, but the final product will be one many can enjoy.

ACKNOWLEDGEMENTS

I extend unbounded gratitude to all those who helped make this book possible.

To anyone who has taken an infographic workshop with me and asked thoughtful questions and offered insightful suggestions, I have learned so much from you. These 10 steps are rooted in your real-world experiences and desire to communicate visually with the world.

To Anne Cosby who would debrief with me after all our infographic workshops about what we heard from participants, what we needed to change, and how we'd make the workshop better next time. Without your partnership, sense of humor, and contributions to this book and growing our line of work in infographics, I'm not sure this book would've come to life.

To Dr. Billie-Jo Grant for planting seeds of inspiration by encouraging our team at Magnolia Consulting to create infographics and present workshops on infographics at the American Evaluation Association annual conferences. This gave me the purpose and focus I needed to fill a gap in the research and evaluation field on a practical process for creating infographics.

To the designers, researchers, and evaluators whose dedication to communicating visual stories through the infographics included in this book allowed me to visually show the 10-step process.

To Kristen Erickson and Lin Chambers of the NASA Science Activation program, Dr. Joelle Clark and the NASA PLANETS project team at Northern Arizona University and partnering organizations, and the evaluation team at Magnolia Consulting, for allowing the PLANETS infographic to serve as the illustrative example for how to create an infographic. Using the PLANETS infographic to demonstrate each of the 10 steps grounds the infographic development process in an authentic and realistic way.

To the experts in the field of data visualization and infographic design who influenced my thinking and understanding in developing the 10-step process, Randy Krum, Cole Nussbaumer Knaflic, Nancy Duarte, David McCandless, Alberto Cairo, and Stephanie Evergreen. As someone who considers herself a non-designer, I remain a life-long learner of the significant contributions you've made to the art of visual communication.

To Helen Salmon, Beth Ginter, and the talented team at SAGE for seeing value in this book and bringing it to an international audience of students and practitioners, particularly in the field of research and evaluation.

I am also very grateful for generous feedback from the previously anonymous SAGE reviewers which helped with the development of this book:

- Marisa Beeble, *Michigan State University*

- Anne C. Campbell, Ph.D., *Middlebury Institute of International Studies*

- Bret D. Cormier, *Southeast Missouri State University*

- Michele Mosco, *Arizona State University*

- Jeffrey Nachtigal, *Cuesta College*

- Kathryn Newcomer, *The George Washington University*

- Kimberly Rios, *Ohio University*

- Jon Ross, Ph.D., *Adler University*

- Daniel J. Svyantek, *Auburn University*

To my Magnolia Consulting family, particularly Catherine Pearson and interns Erica Ross and Jaime Williams, for your contributions, patience, and support.

To my soul family, Clay, Zach, and Wyatt for supporting me in simultaneously running a company and writing a book. Your unconditional love and understanding made this possible. You have always been, and always will be, my raison d'etre.

AUTHOR BIO

Stephanie B. Wilkerson is President of Magnolia Consulting, a woman-owned small business and B Corporation specializing in research and evaluation since 2002. With the aim of "cultivating learning and positive change" through her work at Magnolia, Stephanie takes a use-focused approach to her studies, trainings, and consultation services. She champions infographics as a powerful vehicle for translating data into evidence-based information people can use. As an evaluator, not a graphic designer, she developed the 10 Steps to Creating an Infographic and the Checklist for Reviewing Infographics as practical tools for communicating study findings in a visually impactful way. Stephanie has conducted numerous trainings on the 10-step development process for international audiences in nonprofit organizations, professional membership organizations, and federal agencies within the United States and Canada.

Building on her doctorate from the University of Virginia in Research, Evaluation, and Statistics, she has applied her expertise in program evaluation and qualitative and quantitative methodologies to a broad range of studies at national, state, and local levels. For over two decades, Stephanie has directed randomized controlled trials, quasi-experimental evaluations, and nonexperimental studies funded by the U.S. Department of Education, the Department of Justice, the Department of Labor, the National Science Foundation, the National Aeronautics and Space Administration, top education publishers, and nonprofit organizations. Her nationally recognized studies have given her a deep understanding of clients' information needs, the challenges inherent in working with data, and how to translate study findings into useful information that guides decision making and catalyzes action. Her extensive experience in applied research and evaluation motivates her use of infographics to communicate powerful messages that audiences will remember.

INTRODUCTION TO 10 STEPS TO CREATING INFOGRAPHICS

A Practical Guide for Non-Designers

> **LEARNING OBJECTIVES**
>
> In this chapter, you will learn:
>
> - what characterizes an infographic,
> - different representations of an infographic,
> - why infographics are an effective communication tool,
> - how infographics have been used historically, and
> - uses of infographics in research and evaluation.

Have you ever possessed information that held the potential to improve people's lives, even if in a small way, but you weren't sure how best to communicate it? Maybe you wanted to make people more aware, informed, or engaged about a pressing issue or topic of interest. Perhaps you wanted to catalyze a call to action for change, but you didn't know how to get your message out into a world filled with overwhelming digital noise, distraction, and information. Or possibly, you exhausted your normal communication channels—publications, presentations, emails— and yet, you still didn't reach the audiences you envisioned.

If you have ever wanted to shout from the rooftops with a message for people to hear and remember in a professionally compelling way, then maybe infographics are for you. Infographics are like a visual megaphone that amplifies and broadcasts your message to an ever-expanding audience. When you capture people's attention visually, not only do they see the information, they experience it, and with experience comes understanding. When people understand and remember your message, they are more likely to share it and act on it.

One of the first nationally recognized infographics my company developed shed light on an education problem no one talked about: school employee sexual misconduct (Figure 0.1). After

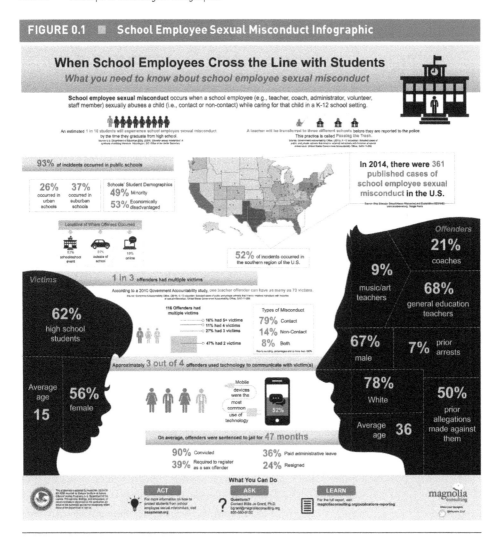

FIGURE 0.1 ■ School Employee Sexual Misconduct Infographic

Source: Stephanie Wilkerson, Anne Cosby, Molly Henschel, Billie-Jo Grant, 2017

conducting an in-depth research study on the topic, my team and I wanted to talk about it, and we needed people to listen. Not only did we need them to listen, we wanted them to understand the results of our study and take action to protect students from harm. When we only had minutes to capture the attention of staff in a U.S. Senator's office and the Office for Civil Rights, as well as broader audiences through email and social media, we knew we had to go visual. Of course, our full report would be accessible, but we were up against competing priorities for people's time, attention, and resources. Through a visual display of our findings, we would remind them why they should care—and act—on the study's results. So we set out to tell the story about a topic no one was talking about through infographics.

As researchers we were proficient in creating data visualizations such as charts and graphs to present statistical findings. We also had experience distilling lengthy reports into executive summaries and one-page reports, but we were relatively new to communicating complex information visually. We weren't graphic designers either, but we were fueled by passion and determination for our research to make a difference, rather than reside in a journal on a shelf. So we followed the 10 Steps for Creating an Infographic and put together a family of infographics to tell the story about school employee sexual misconduct.

We'd love to say those infographics went on to win epic awards, catalyze new legislation that changed the world forever, and prevented all students from harm. That's not quite what happened. Well, one of the infographics won an award for "best poster" out of 400 entries at a national professional conference. More importantly, the infographics got noticed by policymakers, journalists, and advocates across the country. The U.S. Department of Education funded more research on the topic and cited our study. It also informed the decision to add questions about school employee sexual misconduct incidents to the annual Civil Rights Data Collection survey that goes to all public schools. We had inquiries and requests for interviews from journalists across the country wanting to learn more about our study, and who later published stories on the issue, citing our work.

We have been writing highly visual and well-received reports for over 20 years, but not one has gotten as much attention as these infographics. We don't know how many people have actually read the full-length report, but we know the infographics got people's attention, and more people are talking about the problem and taking action.

WHAT IS AN INFOGRAPHIC?

Simply put, an infographic is information communicated visually. It combines information, including data, with design elements to facilitate visual learning (Smiciklas, 2012). An infographic condenses complex information into digestible chunks that a reader can process and understand in a matter of minutes, or even seconds. It does this by telling a compelling story through data visualizations, illustrations, photographs, and images with supporting text (Cairo, 2016; Krum, 2014). Most often we see infographics in print and digital formats found in news articles, magazines, billboards, books, websites, reports, and social media, for example. With the competition for people's attention, enhanced visual elements such as animations, video, and interactions with infographic visualizations are becoming more prevalent, especially online (Lankow et al., 2012).

There are no agreed-upon rules for how much text or how many visuals differentiate an infographic from a visual flyer or single data visualization. People sometimes use the label "infographic" to describe products that appear as text-based flyers or simple data visualizations. For example, the Regional Educational Laboratory (REL) program refers to the four-pager, *Why Do Students' Languages Matter*, as an infographic. It includes appealing visuals, a harmonious color scheme, and subtle cues to demarcate multiple sections of the infographic, and it relies predominantly on text to communicate a story (Figure 0.2).

FIGURE 0.2 ■ *Why Do Students' Languages Matter Infographic*

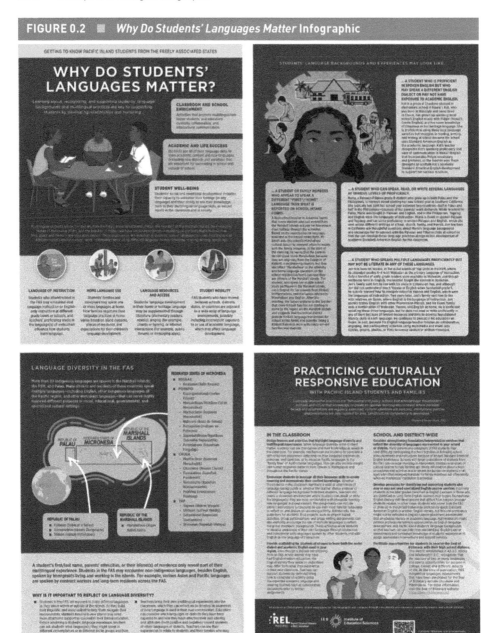

Source: US Department of Education, 2021

In contrast, some people consider a simple data visualization with a visual cue that communicates information as an infographic (Lankow et al., 2012). Interactive dashboards, sometimes referred to as interactive infographics or news applications, engage the audience in viewing data in different ways with minimal supporting text (Cairo, 2016; Nadj et al., 2020). An example includes the COVID-19 maps commonly presented throughout the pandemic beginning in 2020 (Figure 0.3). This interactive dashboard allows the reader to change the information presented in the visual by examining COVID-19 data by state or county. Although interactive dashboards might not communicate an author-driven story, the purpose is to facilitate explanation through interaction based on individuals' own lives, information needs, and interests (Dick, 2013).

The next example is also considered an infographic under the REL program, *Profiles of Certified Teachers Who Graduated From the College of Micronesia-FSM in the Federated States of Micronesia.* The *Profiles of Certified Teachers* infographic primarily consists of visuals with text used to support the visual displays (aside from the reference page). Glancing at the infographic, the reader can discern the story through the visuals with minimal reliance on text. This is different from the *Why Do Students' Languages Matter* example, which uses text to communicate a story, and the COVID–19 interactive map, which uses a single visualization to facilitate interaction-based explanation.

All three of these examples—regardless of what you call them—share similar design elements, such as use of color to promote visual appeal and coherence. They lack extraneous visual

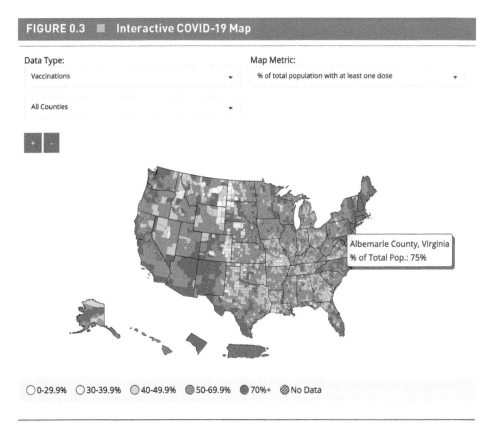

FIGURE 0.3 ■ Interactive COVID-19 Map

Data Type:

Vaccinations

All Counties

Map Metric:

% of total population with at least one dose

Albemarle County, Virginia
% of Total Pop.: 75%

○ 0-29.9% ○ 30-39.9% ○ 40-49.9% ● 50-69.9% ● 70%+ ⊘ No Data

Source: Centers for Disease Control and Prevention and Prevention and Prevention, COVID-19 Integrated County View, 2023

FIGURE 0.4 ■ *Profiles of Certified Teachers in the Federated States of Micronesia Infographic*

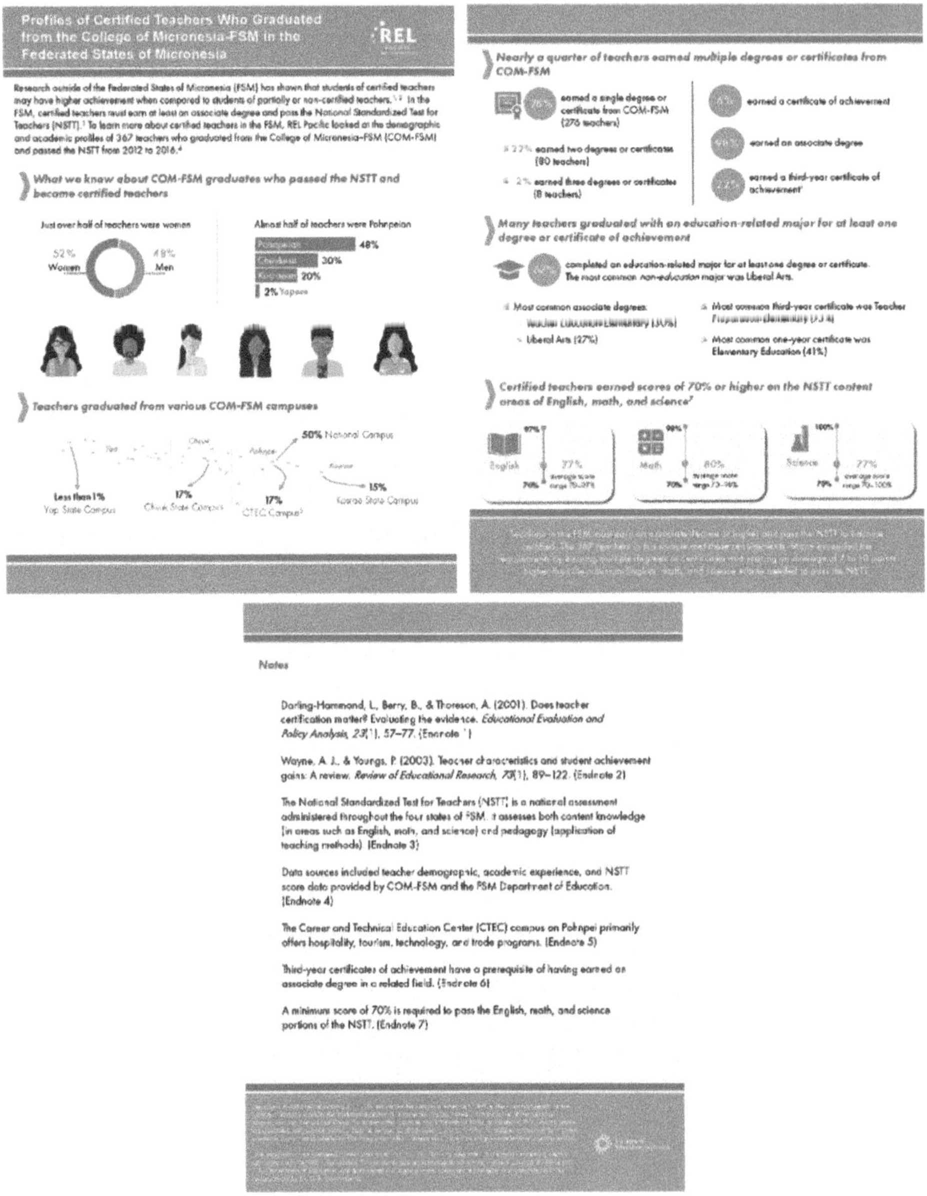

Source: US Department of Education, 2021

noise, and their visual appeal attracts the audience's attention. Information is chunked into sections or segments for the audience to navigate. All three focus the reader's attention on the data, whether it be qualitative data, in the case of the *Why Do Students' Languages Matter* narrative story, or quantitative data presented in the other two examples. The main difference among the three is the use of visuals in relationship to text in communicating an intentional story.

Our approach to creating infographics aims to communicate a visual story with a beginning, middle, and end and a clearly defined purpose for an intended audience. The infographics we encourage through the 10 Steps development process include photographs, illustrations, icons, images, and data visualizations that visually communicate a main message. With our approach, visuals are the primary storyteller in an infographic, with textual information providing supporting details. We include a variety of infographics in this book to illustrate different aspects of visual and infographic design, representing our "visuals show the story" approach to varying degrees.

WHY COMMUNICATE WITH INFOGRAPHICS?

We are overloaded with information and often lack the time to read documents from beginning to end. Text can be laborious to read and comprehend, it can be misinterpreted, and it can disengage the reader. Online audiences will only read 20% of a webpage with more than 600 words (Nielsen, 2018; Weinreich et al., 2008). Visuals combined with text ease understanding, by giving cues that help readers decode the text. When visual content grabs our attention it helps us focus on the information we need. Text presented with visual images improves reader comprehension by up to 89% compared to text presented alone (Clark & Mayer, 2016). As a result, visuals are potentially a more efficient and clear way of communicating than text alone (Dunlap & Lowenthal, 2016).

Vision is our dominant sense. It originated with our survival instinct to help us recognize patterns in the environment that distinguish predators, food, and mates. This instinct is still within us, but instead of scanning for threats or opportunities to help us physically survive, we scan for information. We evolved to constantly scan the environment for patterns that alert us, focus our attention, and help us make decisions. We use our visual sense to sift through information, determine what is most critical for our purposes, and interpret what we see to improve our knowledge, abilities, and decision making (Krum, 2014).

Visuals expedite information processing and increase our capacity to comprehend and synthesize new information. With an estimated 50% to 80% of our brain dedicated to visual processing, visuals help people find the information they need faster than text alone (Djamasbi et al., 2010; Krum, 2014). Whereas our brains decode text through a linear process, it processes information from visual images all at once (Smiciklas, 2012). When people view an image, they encode the information using more representations and associations than with words. This activates multiple neural pathways to support memory (Paivio, 1971).

Visuals create an experience and attract our attention to information, increasing the likelihood that we will remember what we see. Compared to text or oral modes of communication, people are capable of recalling hundreds of pictures, even when only seeing them for a few seconds (Zull, 2002). When text is mixed with images, we remember up to 67% of that information three days later, compared to only 10% of information that is presented as text alone (Figure 6; Beegel, 2014; Medina, 2008). This is commonly referred to as the Picture Superiority Effect (Nelson et al., 1977), and its relevance to learning cannot be understated.

An estimated 65% of people are visual learners, meaning we learn best when we can see visual representation of an idea or concept (Zopf et al., 2004). Visuals can assist with cognitive processing by providing context or metaphor, and when used effectively, can help people understand abstract and complex information when they may be unfamiliar with the concept. From an instructional and educational perspective, presenting visual explanations facilitates more understanding of new content than presenting verbal or written explanations alone (Bobek & Tversky, 2016). Generally, learners are more likely to remember and understand instructional and informational messages that are highly visual.

HOW HAVE WE USED INFOGRAPHICS TO COMMUNICATE?

In one form or another, people have communicated information visually for thousands of years (Figure 0.5). While cave drawings dating back to 30,000 BC might not resemble how we think about modern infographics, our ancestors used symbolic paintings to communicate stories of significant events, rituals, and ways of life (Featherstone, 2014). From 3,000 BC, Egyptians used hieroglyphics consisting of symbols and icons (pictures of objects used as the words for those objects) to create a visual language for communication. Cave drawings and hieroglyphics served as communication and historical perseveration mechanisms for these societies that created them ages ago. Today, we still rely on our interpretations of these visual stories to understand the cultural, social, and religious significance of our human evolution and history.

FIGURE 0.5 ■ Picture Superiority Effect

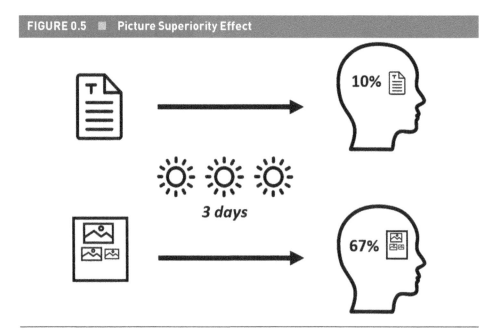

Source: Stephanie Wilkerson and Anne Cosby, 2023

Over time, our purpose for communicating information visually through infographics became more explanatory and instructional to educate others. We see this through examples such as Nicole d'Orseme's explanatory graphs for how to measure a moving object in 1350 or Leonardo da Vinci's illustrative guide to the human anatomy in 1510 (Babb, 2003; Kemp, 2007). William Playfair pioneered data visualization by using charts and graphs to explain numeric data in 1786 (Otten et al., 2015). By the 1860s, Charles Minard created a single infographic to distill complex data into a visual depiction of Napoleon's 1812 failed attempt to invade Russia (Tufte, 1983). These are examples of how philosophers, artists, scientists, and engineers used visuals as a teaching tool to help convey complex information.

Infographics have also been used to communicate important information related to public health issues and practices. Using an infographic map, Dr. John Snow demonstrated that local, unclean water was the source of an aggressive cholera outbreak in 1854, which provided health officials with the evidence necessary to end the epidemic by demonstrating it was not airborne (Koch, 2005; Tufte, 1997). In 1856, Florence Nightingale used a type of pie chart in an infographic to visually show how deaths could have been avoided during the Crimean War. As a result of her infographics, conditions in military hospitals improved (Smiciklas, 2012). In more recent times, infographics have been used as an education and public outreach strategy for communicating good health practices across the world.

Communicating data and information through the use of infographics ensures audiences with varying levels of education and background knowledge receive a consistent message and can help overcome language barriers (Featherstone, 2014; McCrorie et al., 2016). Communicating critical health information through visual images can be particularly important in nonliterate countries with poor health conditions. In the early twentieth century, Otto Neurath produced many infographics addressing a variety of social, political, and health topics. These included his isotype array graphic to illustrate the ratio of side effects due to statin usage. This graphic was primarily used to communicate potentially lifesaving information to people with poor literacy or numeracy skills (McCrorie et al., 2016). Infographics are also effectively used in the areas of health education and public outreach by presenting complex health information in an easy-to-understand manner. For example, infographics are used to facilitate understanding of causes, risks, and treatments of disease and can be shared broadly for public health uses (Balkac & Ergun, 2018). As such, The Center for Disease Control has used infographics as an effective communication tool to increase awareness about health issues and practices.

With the shift to the information age in the 1970s, infographics became a more mainstream communication tool. This is partly attributed to graphic artists, such as Alfred Leete, who immigrated to America from Europe and brought their design expertise from the sciences and social sciences into the communications field (Dick, 2015). From 1982 to 1991, journalists began to introduce a significant change in the appearance of newspapers as they began telling stories with drawings in addition to photos and text (Utt & Pasternack, 1993). During this time, more and more front-page space was dedicated to graphic displays, with the average newspaper containing more than four infographics per issue (Utt & Pasternack, 1993). Despite questions of accuracy and analysis methods used in newspapers, this effort paved the way for other publications to develop practices that support more complex yet accessible visualizations (Otten et al., 2015). In 1983, Edward Tufte published one of the first books on the visual display of quantitative information, which influenced the field of data visualization.

FIGURE 0.6 ■ Visual History of Infographics

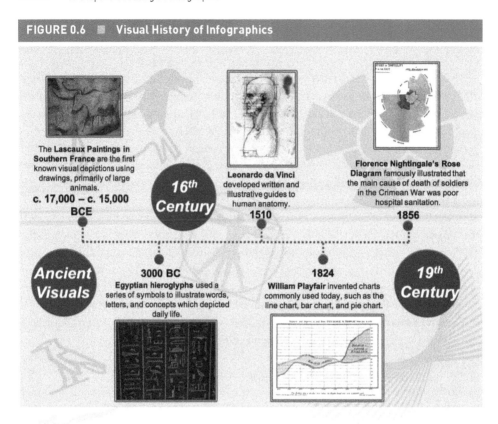

Source: Stephanie B. Wilkerson and Anne Cosby (2022) with images from Wikimedia (2001, 2009, 2011, 2013, 2014, 2020).

In the current age of social media, there has been an increased focus on creating and disseminating infographics. Google Trends data for "infographic" and "infographics" show virtually zero searches until 2010, when the number of searches for these terms increased dramatically (Featherstone, 2014). This newfound interest in infographics reflects the availability of web tools for creating user-generated graphics. Web-based design products (e.g., Piktochart, Ease. ly, Visual.ly, etc.) provide amateur designers with the ability to create their own infographics, and media sites that rely on user-generated content (e.g., Twitter and Pinterest) allow for rapid dissemination on social networks (Featherstone, 2014).

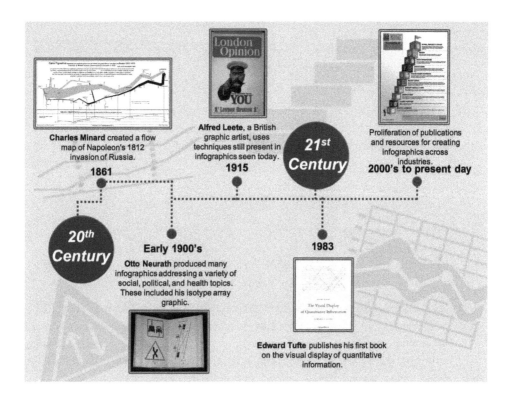

HOW CAN WE USE INFOGRAPHICS IN RESEARCH AND EVALUATION?

We can conduct highly credible studies that employ the most sophisticated analytical techniques, but if we can't communicate complex findings in a way people can understand and use, then we fail to actualize the potential of research and evaluation to improve society. Most often, we've communicated evaluation results through comprehensive evaluation reports, executive summaries, and oral presentations. What we noticed is that very few people actually read the report from beginning to end and most people refer to the executive summary.

Infographics can be used in several ways throughout the process of conducting a research or evaluation study:

- **Study planning** — Infographics can present study information in an unintimidating, user-friendly manner; help build understanding of the study process; and provide an easy way to share planning details with those unable to attend meetings.

- **Study recruitment** — In recruitment, infographics can engage potential study participants; give basic information on benefits, expectations, and study activities; and direct interested candidates in finding more information.

- **Study orientation** — At orientation, an infographic can present important information about study participation and provide a summary of the information that participants can easily refer to throughout the study.

- **Progress monitoring** — Infographics are a great way to orient a group to the history and progress of a study over time. The visual helps stakeholders organize a lot of information about study activities in a meaningful way that shows what's been accomplished and what remains to be done.

- **Reporting and dissemination** — Infographics can be used in addition to or in place of an executive summary, depending on intended use. A longer version that includes all key findings can serve as a report summary; infographic presentations are easily shared online and through social media, encouraging wide dissemination. An infographic poster presented at professional meetings or conferences is also an effective way to disseminate study findings to large audiences.

STEP 1: IDENTIFY YOUR AUDIENCE (THE "WHO")

The power of an infographic lies in its ability to catalyze change. Through a compelling story and a call to action, an infographic can inform or transform its audience. Yet the audience won't experience change in understanding or take any action if the infographic's message doesn't connect with what matters to them.

By visually displaying information, infographics connect with their audience on both intellectual and emotional levels (Smiciklas, 2012). When an infographic's message resonates emotionally with an audience, they are more likely to recall the information conveyed and take action (Medina, 2014; Norman, 2004). Therefore, understanding the information needs, priorities, and interests of the infographic's audience is a critical first step for creating a powerful visual message.

UNDERSTANDING THE "WHO" OF AN INFOGRAPHIC

Creating an infographic begins with knowing your audience. The infographic, after all, is for them, not for you. As professionals conducting studies and working with data, we sometimes believe that all the information generated from studies has pressing value and importance. But to a specific audience, some pieces of information hold more value than others. For example, consider a study that focuses on a particular program. The information from the study that program sponsors need for guiding future funding decisions will be different than the information that program developers need for making program improvements. Program providers might need information about how to successfully deliver and implement the program, whereas potential participants might want to know about the experiences and outcomes of past program participants. When we take into account how intended audiences, or stakeholders, will be using study results, we can ensure that our infographics respond to their information needs.

DETERMINING THE AUDIENCE FOR AN INFOGRAPHIC

Key audiences for an infographic might include those who invested in the program or study, as well as those who stand to benefit from program outcomes (Figure 1.1). Consider who has the most funds, time, or resources invested in the study. The investor audience could include study funders, program sponsors, program developers, and program providers. Investors also include stakeholders who are personally or emotionally invested in program outcomes—perhaps those who have the greatest to gain or lose based on study results. Program beneficiaries could include current and future program participants. Investors and beneficiaries typically are audiences directly involved in supporting the program or the study. Investors and beneficiaries might also receive study results in other forms, such as a written report, findings summary, or presentation, so consider the added value of presenting these audiences with an infographic. Often, an infographic allows these audiences to communicate with other stakeholders about the program and therefore is an effective dissemination strategy.

FIGURE 1.1 ■ Identify Your Infographic Audience

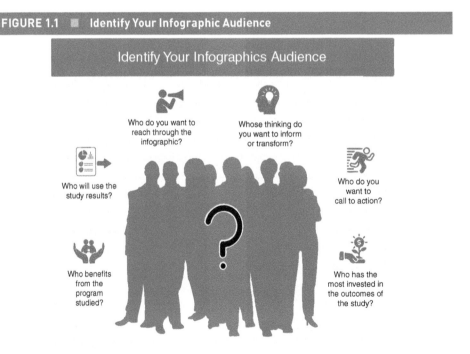

An infographic can reach broader audiences as well, perhaps audiences who won't have access to the study report and who are unaware of the program under study. You might want to inform them about the study results to increase their awareness, build their understanding, and perhaps call them to take action. These audiences could include, for example, the general public, community members, parents and families, potential investors, social justice advocates, and policymakers.

If your study is client-funded, talk with them about who they see as the audience for the study results. Your client might have a communication plan already in place that specifies which audiences or stakeholder groups should receive what information. Alternatively, your study might have a reporting and dissemination plan that outlines the communication method you will use with each stakeholder group (Hutchinson, 2017). When you and your clients incorporate infographics into the design phase of a study, they become part of a larger communication and dissemination strategy for reaching intended audiences. In this case, there likely is a planned budget for infographics, which will influence the number of different infographics that can be created for various audiences. Alternatively, knowing that there is a budget for only one infographic will help you prioritize which audience is most important to reach.

IDENTIFYING THE INFORMATION NEEDS AND INTERESTS OF THE AUDIENCE

Once you identify who the audience is, you'll want to delve into understanding what they care about and how the study is relevant to their information needs and interests. Most key audience members will care about whether the program was effective in accomplishing its intended outcomes, but you can't assume that is all they will want to know. Asking your client and study audience representatives about their information needs and interests during this step will anchor future decisions in the infographic development process (see Know Your Audience: Questions to Ask).

BOX 1.1. KNOW YOUR AUDIENCE: QUESTIONS TO ASK

During Steps 1–3 of developing an infographic, you will want to connect with your client and audience groups to understand their information needs, priorities, and interests. Here are some guiding questions to consider.

1. Who is your audience for this study?
2. What information from the study would be most relevant to your audience? What information matters to them?
3. How might the audience use information from the study?
4. Who will receive information about the study, and how will they receive it?
5. For which audience members would an infographic be an appropriate communication tool?

6. What background knowledge does the audience have about the topic? Are they aware of the study? Do they have background in evaluation or research?
7. What is the audience's cultural background, and how might that inform their receptivity to information and visual design choices for the infographic, including color and image associations?
8. How would you share an infographic with your audience?
9. If there is one thing the audience takes away from the infographic, what would it be?
10. What do you hope will change for the audience as a result of reading the infographic?

Study Funders and Program Sponsors

Program investors, beneficiaries, and general public members might have different information needs from the same study, and an effective infographic should take into account these needs (Torres et al., 2005). For example, those that fund a study but have no ties to the program itself, such as a federal agency or nonprofit organization, might care about the rigor of the study design and the validity of its findings (Figure 1.2). They want audiences to have confidence in the results from the study they funded. Program sponsors want to know the program is worth the investment. They also might need to make decisions about continuing program funding or scaling up implementation. Future study funders or program sponsors might want to know if a program or initiative has evidence of effectiveness or shows promise and therefore would be worth funding (Wilkerson & Haden, 2014).

Program Developers and Providers

Program developers and providers are probably the audiences with the most knowledge and experience with a program or initiative, and therefore, they are heavily invested in its implementation and outcomes. Program developers often are interested in recommendations for improvement and in data that will inform program modifications. If the program didn't accomplish the intended outcomes, they might want to know what aspects of the design could be improved. If the program accomplished intended outcomes, developers might want to know if there are program design features that could be replicated for new programs.

In addition to information related to a program's design, program developers and program providers might be interested in study findings about program delivery. They might be interested in knowing the conditions and supports for successful implementation. They might also want to know about the feasibility of implementation in different contexts and if program providers were able to implement the program as intended. Program providers might be interested in practical information and best practices for ensuring successful implementation, as well as lessons learned and implications for future practice (Wilkerson & Haden, 2014).

Program Participants

Infographics that capture the experiences, perceptions, and voices of participants can tell a compelling story about the importance of a program. Program participants might look to an

FIGURE 1.2 ■ Audience Information Needs

Examples of Audience Information Needs

Audience	Information Needs
Study funders	Evidence of effectiveness Validity of results
Program sponsors	Evidence of effectiveness Potential to scale up implementation Funding continuation
Program developers	Evidence of effectiveness Feasibility of implementation Conditions and supports for implementation Data to inform program modifications Recommendations for program improvement
Program providers	Evidence of effectiveness Lessons learned and best practices for implementation How to implement with fidelity in local context
Program participants	Participant experience Participant changes and impact
General public	Description of topic and problem addressed Why it matters; reason to care about it What can be done and the benifit of taking action
Policymakers and policy advocates	Description of topic and problem addressed Prevalence and salience of problem addressed Evidence of effectiveness Policy implications and recommendations
Evaluators and researchers	Study design and methods Methodological approach, challenges, and lessons learned Study results

infographic to accurately represent their experiences in the program or study. If the infographic doesn't reflect their experiences, participants are unlikely to see much value or credibility in the information presented. Program participants might also be interested in knowing about the broader program impacts for all participants.

General Public

The general public is a common audience for infographics because an infographic's purpose often is to raise public awareness of the problem or issue that the program is intended to address. To accomplish this goal, the infographic needs to provide members of the general public with information about the topic of study, the problem addressed, and how it was addressed. The public will also want to know the benefit to them for caring about the program or taking action based on the study's results.

Policymakers and Policy Advocates

Policymakers and policy advocates might be unaware of the program or initiative being studied, but they are likely to have some awareness of the topic or problem being addressed. They might be interested in the prevalence and salience of a problem because they make decisions that affect communities and large populations. The evidence supporting study findings is important, but policymakers are often most interested in understanding the implications of study findings for creating or modifying policies. They need clear and concise policy recommendations that are within their sphere of influence.

Evaluators and Researchers

Fellow evaluators and researchers are also potential audiences for infographics as part of a professional community of learners. In this context, interest could relate to study design and methods, methodological approaches for complex programs, and challenges and lessons learned during study implementation. Aside from an interest in study methods, evaluators and researchers will also be interested in study results.

The information needs, priorities, and interests of infographic audiences may be similar to the general needs of the study's audience. If you identified your audience and their information needs at the onset of designing a research or evaluation study, then the study's findings should respond to those needs. When a study is complete, the focus becomes selecting the communication method that is most appropriate for responding to the needs of a particular audience. Infographics are an effective way of disseminating information to a range of audiences, and they might be preferable over a written report or other communication method for audiences who

- won't have access to the full report;
- have limited time or interest in reading a full report;
- need a "hook" that resonates with them, connects them to the value and importance of the study, and motivates them to learn more through the full report;
- need a portable and easy-to-share method for disseminating findings to broader audiences, such as through social media and email; and
- want a visually engaging way to embed program information or findings on a website.

Identifying the audience for an infographic involves knowing their information needs and confirming that an infographic is an appropriate communication method to respond to those needs.

ADDRESSING MULTIPLE AUDIENCES

When there are several potential audiences for an infographic, it can be challenging to determine if an infographic can respond to the needs and interests of all of them. Sometimes multiple audiences will have shared information needs and interests, but they will use the same information in an infographic differently. Our infographic, *K–12 School Employee Sexual Misconduct: Lessons Learned From Title IX Policy Implementation*, summarized key study findings relevant to multiple audiences. However, the findings had different implications for each audience (i.e., researchers, educators, state and federal leaders, and higher education faculty), therefore, we listed separate action items for each audience group in the infographic's conclusion (Figure 1.3). This was an efficient and cost-effective way of using one infographic to address the needs and interests of multiple audiences.

Conversely, you might find that multiple audiences have distinctly different information needs and interests, which makes creating one infographic that will satisfy everyone impractical.

FIGURE 1.3 ■ Example Infographic With Multiple Audiences

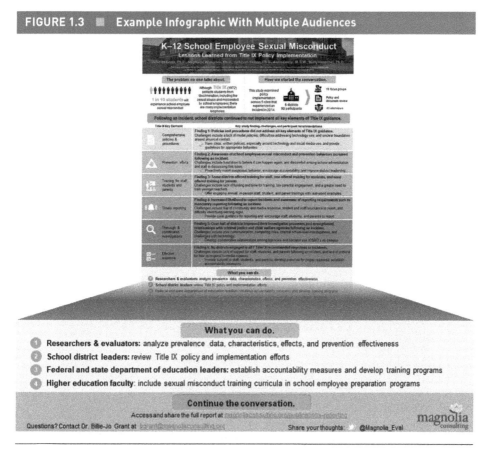

Source: Stephanie Wilkerson, Anne Cosby, Molly Henschel, Billie-Jo Grant, 2023

If there is time and budget for creating more than one infographic, you can develop distinctly different infographics for each audience and purpose. Alternatively, you can create a family of complementary infographics that together tell a comprehensive story about the program or topic. In this case, consider creating a replicable infographic design template that you can populate with information and visuals relevant to each audience. If funding prevents developing multiple infographics for various audiences, then perhaps create one infographic that addresses the information needs held by the audience you most want to reach.

GET TO KNOW YOUR AUDIENCE

Many evaluators and researchers design studies to address a problem or an area of need for a given population. Even if you designed the evaluation or research study with an audience's needs in mind, communicating with the audience requires an additional understanding of their culture, background knowledge, and intended use of study information (Figure 1.4). This goes

FIGURE 1.4 ■ Get to Know Your Audience

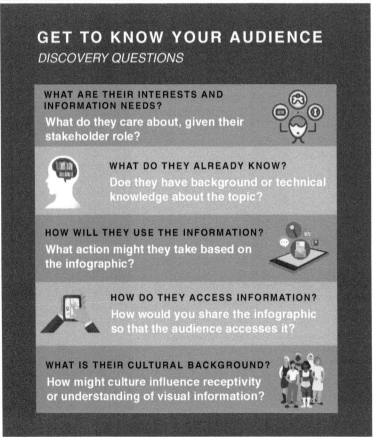

beyond identifying a need or rationale for conducting the study. It's about putting yourself in the shoes of your audience—the people who will interpret and derive meaning from your infographic.

To the extent possible, you will want to understand and take into account the cultural background of your audience when developing the infographic. Improving your cultural awareness of the characteristics, beliefs, and values your audience holds related to gender, race, ethnicity, religion, disability, age, social class, and profession will help inform the design decisions you make in later infographic design steps. Ultimately, you want to create a culturally sensitive infographic that is appropriate for your audience and how they might perceive and interpret the visual information in your infographic.

You'll also want to consider how much the audience already knows about the topic of the infographic. Primary stakeholders, such as program sponsors, developers, providers, and participants, will likely know more about the study focus, whereas secondary or tertiary stakeholders, such as the general public, policymakers, or other evaluators and researchers, might know less. Understanding what background knowledge the audience brings to the table will help you determine the type and level of descriptive program information you need to include in the infographic. This is the information the audience needs in order to understand the infographic's central message.

You'll also want to take into account how much the audience knows about the technical aspects of the infographic's data and study information. This influences the tone and language you use in the infographic. An audience with a technical background in research and evaluation methods might expect to see extensive statistical documentation in an infographic, such as effect sizes, p-values, and sample sizes. But presenting data in this way could make it hard for nontechnical audiences to understand the infographic's message. An infographic needs to speak the language of the audience in order to keep their attention and promote understanding.

CONSIDER HOW THE AUDIENCE WILL ACCESS THE INFOGRAPHIC

The local context in which the audience will access and use the infographic has implications for the design elements and dissemination methods you choose during later steps of infographic development. Will the audience access the infographic by visiting a website, following social media, reading an email or newsletter, participating in an electronic mailing list, or receiving a report? You'll want to think about the audience's access methods and identify any potential barriers or limitations to access, such as Internet connectivity or social media use. Where the infographic will "live," such as in a blog post, on a website, in a report, or on social media, will affect the size of the infographic. Whether the audience will view the infographic in a print or online format influences design elements such as color, font size, and page size as well as other design specifications (see Steps 5 and 6 for more on infographic layout and design).

BOX 1.2. STEP 1 DESIGN CHALLENGE 2

DESIGN CHALLENGE: WHAT IF I DON'T KNOW INFORMATION ABOUT THE AUDIENCE?

Determining the information needs and interests of an infographic audience isn't always easy. You'll have direct access to some audiences, such as program providers and participants, who might also be involved in the study. Other audiences, such as community members or the general public, might be less accessible and more challenging to understand. *So how can you determine the information needs and interests of your audience when they aren't clear?*

Ask! The best way to know your audience is to contact members of the group directly. These could be primary stakeholders for the study—that is, people who stand to benefit from or are impacted by study results. You'll also want to engage these stakeholder representatives to review your infographic during later development steps, so it's best to involve them early in the process. If you don't have direct access to representatives of your target audience, ask your client, study funder, or program sponsor. They should have a good understanding of the audiences they serve and intend to reach.

Research! Visit the websites and social media accounts of groups, associations, and organizations that the audience might belong to. What they post represents what matters to them. Learn about their mission, their purpose, and the difference they want to make through what they offer. You can also scan research and evaluation literature for needs assessments, market research, or other studies involving the target audience to see if these studies shed any light on the audience's needs, interests, and priorities.

BOX 1.3. PLANETS ILLUSTRATIVE EXAMPLE

PLANETS ILLUSTRATIVE EXAMPLE—IDENTIFYING THE AUDIENCE

The Planetary Learning That Advances the Nexus of Engineering, Technology, and Science (PLANETS) project provides educators in out-of-school time (OST) settings with curriculum guides that include National Aeronautics and Space Administration (NASA) planetary science content aligned to National Science Standards. With funding from NASA's Science Activation five-year grant program, researchers at the Northern Arizona University Center for Science Teaching and Learning (NAU CSTL) lead the PLANETS project in collaboration with scientists at the U.S. Geological Survey (USGS) Astrogeology Science Center and researchers at the Museum of Science, Boston (MOS).

As part of the grant, external evaluators at Magnolia Consulting, LLC, conducted an evaluation study to measure project implementation and outcomes. Key evaluation stakeholders, including PLANETS project partners and NASA Science Activation program administrators, received a comprehensive report on the multiyear formative and summative evaluation. Because disseminating the PLANETS products and study findings was a key project objective, OST educators, who were the intended users of the PLANETS products, seemed like an appropriate audience for the infographic.

What did we know about OST educators? Based on OST educator participants in the evaluation study, OST educators worked in informal education settings such as museums, science centers, and after-school youth clubs, many of which served minority and underrepresented youth. They would have been interested in educational materials that engage learners in hands-on interactive content that reinforced or expanded upon the educational content learners received in formal education settings. Because their time with learners was limited, they needed access to evidence-based materials shown to benefit learners in OST settings. They might have also wanted to know if curriculum materials were appropriate for their OST setting and easy to implement. They could use the information presented in an infographic to determine if the PLANETS curriculum guides would be feasible to implement and beneficial to their OST learners. OST educators would have had varying levels of education, represented different cultural backgrounds, and served diverse populations of OST learners. OST educators typically would not have had technical knowledge of education research and statistics, but they could have had an understanding of general STEM educational content since many OST programs focus on STEM topics and occur within science centers and museums. OST educators would access information digitally and online, and the infographic could also serve as a companion to the PLANETS evaluation report.

> **PLANETS Infographic Audience:**
> Out-of-school time educators in science, technology, engineering, and mathematics (STEM) settings.

NOW IT'S YOUR TURN!

Try different ways of identifying and learning about audiences:

- Find an infographic online at Cool Infographics (https://coolinfographics.com/) or Canva (https://www.canva.com/learn/best-infographics/). After viewing the infographic, is it clear who the intended audience is? Why or why not?

- Think of a charitable organization that serves members of your community (for example, youth, senior citizens, homeless individuals). If a study measured the impact of the organization's outreach to the community members they serve, who might read an infographic presenting information from the study? What might the different audiences be interested in knowing about the services community members receive and why?

- If you are studying a program, who are the audiences who might care about the study's results? Consider the questions in Figure 1.1 to learn as much about your audience as possible.

RESOURCES

Check it out!

- Nancy Duarte's **Seven Questions to Knowing Your Audience** in *slide:ology: The Art and Science of Creating Great Presentations* (2008).

- Kylie Hutchinson's **Principles for More Effective Reporting** in *A Short Primer on Innovative Evaluation Reporting* (2017).

2

STEP 2: CLARIFY THE PURPOSE (THE "WHY")

LEARNING OBJECTIVES

In Step 2, you will learn how to

- clarify the purpose of your infographic,

- frame an infographic's purpose as an intended outcome for your audience, and

- work with multiple purposes for an infographic

Information is a means to an end. As consumers, we *access* information for various purposes, such as education, entertainment, motivation, and advancement. As providers, we *present* information for the purpose of achieving similar types of results. With a clear purpose, we can communicate information visually using infographics to achieve a desired result.

Once you identify your audience and understand their information interests and needs to the extent possible, the next step is to articulate a clear purpose for your infographic. In other words, what do you hope to accomplish through the infographic? An infographic's purpose is the change you hope to catalyze in your audience. This could be a change in your audience's awareness, understanding, interests, or behaviors, for example. Whatever the purpose, it should be clear in your mind as you develop the infographic.

DETERMINING THE "WHY" OF AN INFOGRAPHIC

In Step 1, you identified your audience's information interests and needs. Now consider how they might use the information to meet their interests and needs. The purpose of your infographic should align to your audience's information interests and needs.

Think of an infographic's purpose as the intended outcome for your audience. Where we can get off track is framing an intended outcome as something we accomplish. Presenting, providing, sharing, and distributing information visually are not outcomes for your audience.

Although presenting information visually might seem like an end goal in itself, it is an action that you take as an infographic developer. To identify the intended outcome for your audience, consider *why* you are presenting the information visually to them (Smiciklas, 2012).

In research and evaluation, we often use logic models to distinguish between actions and outcomes. We can apply a similar thought process to determining the intended outcome, or purpose, of an infographic by using "*if-then*" statements. *If* the infographic presents this information, *then* my audience will experience this as a result. This process will help you disentangle an outcome you might see for yourself versus the change you hope to catalyze for your audience through the infographic. Using action verbs to articulate intended actions and outcomes helps frame what your infographic will present and what outcome will result (Figure 2.1). The difference, however, is that the verbs for intended actions (e.g., share, describe, inform, present) represent "doing," and the verbs for intended outcomes (e.g., increase, improve, deepen, enhance) represent how your audience is "changing." As you determine the purpose of your infographic, be sure it represents the intended outcome for your audience.

FIGURE 2.1 ■ Identifying Your Infographic's Purpose

Identifying Your Infographic's purpose	
From ACTION ------▶ To OUTCOME	
If the infographic does this...	... the audience will experience this result.
Describe program activities and participant experiences	Increase awareness of what a program offers
Present data about positive program perceptions	Increase interest in learning more about a program
Share findings about program implementation	Improve understanding of program implementation
Present data about program outcomes	Use data to inform decision making
Provide evidence that a program works	Increase confidence that investment in a program is worthwhile.
Present recommendations for program improvement	Enhance understanding of ways to improve the program

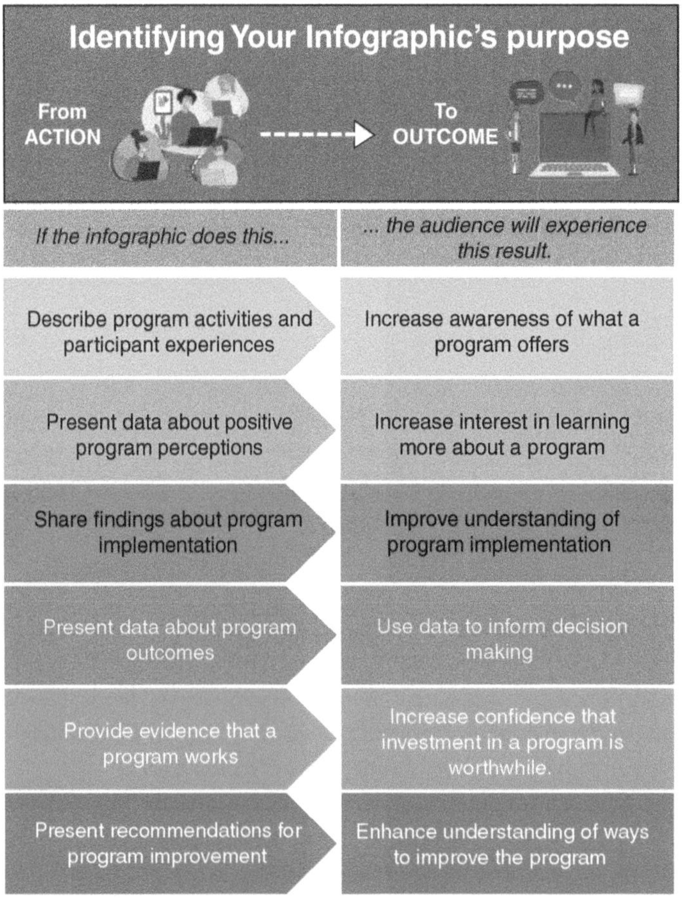

AN INFOGRAPHIC'S PURPOSE WHEN PART OF A STUDY

As evaluators and researchers, we design studies based on a study purpose. To determine a study's purpose, we identify stakeholders, their information needs, and how they will use study results (Gilliam et al., 2002). In developing study questions and a purpose statement, we consider what stakeholders would want to know from a study. We then align our data collection methods, analytical techniques, and reporting to our study purpose so that we can accomplish what we intended from the beginning (Yarbrough et al., 2010).

In many ways, an infographic is an extension of a study's purpose as it is one form of communicating information about a study. Both your study purpose and infographic purpose should be grounded in the information interests and needs of your audience (stakeholders). If you have a clearly articulated study purpose, then the purpose of your infographic should align to it. Your infographic serves as a mechanism for achieving the study's purpose (Dunlap & Lowenthal, 2016).

CLARIFYING PURPOSE MATTERS

Being exceptionally clear about your infographic's purpose and ensuring subsequent design decisions align to your purpose are keys to making your infographic a powerful communication tool. A clearly articulated purpose guides the development of an infographic in future steps. It helps you determine what information is relevant and should be included in the infographic. For example, the infographic's purpose during Step 3 will inform the message your infographic conveys. In Step 4, it will ensure the data and visualizations you select for your infographic represent the information necessary to achieve the infographic's purpose. In Steps 5 and 6, you will select design elements that reinforce the purpose of the infographic.

BOX 2.1. STEP 2 DESIGN CHALLENGE

DESIGN CHALLENGE: WHAT IF THERE ARE MULTIPLE PURPOSES FOR AN INFOGRAPHIC?

You might face the challenge of creating an infographic to accomplish multiple purposes based on the information needs of one or more audiences. *What can you do if you are limited to creating just one infographic to serve multiple purposes?*

Review each purpose and determine if they are equally important. If they all seem equally important, prioritize them based on the following:

- The type of change in your audience you or your client consider to be most important. For instance, increasing an audience's understanding of program outcomes through the infographic might be more important than increasing their understanding about program implementation.

- The extent to which each purpose supports the larger purpose of the study. If there is one purpose that aligns most directly with the study's purpose, that might be the one to select.

- Look at the audience for each purpose you identified. Determine if a particular audience holds more stake in the information for the infographic than another audience. Focusing the infographic on the purpose for this audience might be a priority. For example, a key stakeholder group is future program participants, and the purpose of an infographic for them is to increase their interest and enrollment in the program. Another stakeholder group is program implementers, and the purpose of an infographic for them is to increase the efficiency and effectiveness of program delivery. Enrolling future program participants might be the priority that can best be accomplished through an infographic, whereas a report or presentation geared toward providing program implementers with improvement feedback might be more effective.

Determine if any of the purposes for the infographic could be just as effectively accomplished through other communication and reporting methods. For example, a report might elaborate on the information about program implementation. Blogs or social media posts might be just as effective in increasing awareness about program activities and offerings. Presentations to program developers might be just as effective, if not more so, for communicating recommendations for program improvement.

Attempt addressing multiple purposes in one infographic. It might be that the same visualization can serve multiple purposes for various audiences. If page length isn't an issue, you can also create a longer infographic that includes all the information necessary to accomplish multiple purposes of the infographic.

BOX 2.2. CLARIFY THE PURPOSE

PLANETS ILLUSTRATIVE EXAMPLE—CLARIFY THE PURPOSE

In Step 1, we identified the infographic's audience as out-of-school time (OST) educators because they are the intended users of the PLANETS curriculum units. We also surmised that they could be interested in information about the ease of implementing PLANETS curriculum units and their benefit to OST learners (Haden & Peery, 2021). We knew from the evaluation report that the PLANETS study included various findings related to OST educator implementation of the curriculum units and associated educator and learner outcomes.

There could have been multiple purposes of the PLANETS infographic for OST educators. One purpose could have been to increase the awareness of future OST educators about the

PLANETS curriculum units, their activities, and implementation requirements. Another purpose could have been to inform potential OST educators about the perceptions, experiences, and outcomes of the OST educators who participated in the evaluation study. A third purpose could have been to improve OST educators' understanding of student outcomes associated with participating in the PLANETS activities. Each purpose would result in a distinctive infographic because the ensuing story to achieve each infographic's purpose would have been based on different data and information. It would have been difficult to accomplish all of these purposes through a single infographic, while still making the story concise, compelling, and memorable.

We then considered which purpose best supported the key project objectives. While a key project objective was to disseminate the curriculum units to a national audience of science, technology, engineering, and mathematics (STEM) OST educators, ultimately the goal was to engage learners in collaborative problem-solving through an engineering design process to build learners' habits of mind and improve their attitudes toward engineering. As such, we decided that the purpose of the infographic should focus on learner outcomes. Learner outcomes would be of interest to multiple stakeholders, such as PLANETS project team members and NASA program administrators as well as OST educators. Therefore, we intended that the infographic would increase OST educators' understanding of the learner outcomes resulting from implementation of the PLANETS curricular units. In turn, we believed that with a better understanding of the benefits to learners, OST educators would be interested in accessing and using the PLANETS curriculum units in their OST settings.

> **PLANETS Infographic Purpose:**
> To increase OST educators' understanding of the learner outcomes resulting from implementation of the PLANETS curricular units.

NOW IT'S YOUR TURN!

Try different ways of identifying and learning about an infographic's purpose:

- Find an infographic online and see if you can determine what the purpose of the infographic is (for example, Cool Infographics https://coolinfographics.com/ or Canva https://www.canva.com/learn/best-infographics/). Could the infographic serve multiple purposes? In what ways? If you are unable to discern a clear purpose, what would you change to make it clearer?

- If you are studying a program, consider the audience you identified in Step 1. Now, think about the change you want to catalyze in your audience to determine your infographic's purpose. How would you frame the intended outcome for your audience?

RESOURCES

Check it out!

- Nancy Duarte's **Seven Questions to Knowing Your Audience** in *slide:ology: The Art and Science of Creating Great Presentations* (2008).

- Kylie Hutchinson's **Principles for More Effective Reporting** in *A Short Primer on Innovative Evaluation Reporting* (2017).

- Center for Disease Control and Prevention's Evaluation Reporting: A Guide to Help Ensure Use of Evaluation Findings: https://www.cdc.gov/dhdsp/docs/evaluation_reporting_guide.pdf

STEP 3: CREATE THE STORY (THE "WHAT")

LEARNING OBJECTIVES

In Step 3, you will learn how to

- craft an engaging title for an infographic,

- create an introduction for your infographic that primes the reader for your central message,

- develop your central message by identifying the main and secondary points and supporting details you want to communicate to your audience,

- conclude your infographic with a call to action that reinforces the infographic's purpose, and

- cite the sources of your infographic to support its credibility.

Visual stories can attract our attention, draw us in, and evoke an affective response to what we see so we will remember it (McGaugh, 2013). When a storyline uses visual images to help the reader navigate complex content, the reader is more likely to understand the central message (Nielsen, J., 2018; Weinreich et al., 2008). Because visuals make more of a lasting impression on us than text alone, presenting the visuals in a connected and coherent manner through a story enhances our ability to recall meaning (Knaflic, 2015; Paivio, 1971).

With so much competition for our attention, telling a story through an infographic can be a powerful communication method when done right. Some infographics present alluring information and data visualizations that attract our attention and draw us in. They impress us by their sheer graphic artistry and visual displays. But their impact stops there. Once we drill down into the content and try to make sense of it, we find we are lost in a sea of hypnotic visual distractions. There is no storyline that connects the chunks of information to reveal a central message. Sometimes what we see conjures questions and confusion, rather than clarification.

This renders us feeling visually impressed, but cognitively empty. The difference between these infographics and a powerful infographic: the story.

CREATING THE "WHAT" OF AN INFOGRAPHIC

In Step 3, you create your infographic's story, which is what you need to share with your audience to achieve the purpose you defined in Step 2. It is the substance of an infographic. A powerful story connects with your audience and conveys an evidence-based and compelling message. Elements of an infographic story include an engaging title, an introduction that provides the foundational information the audience needs to grasp the central message, the message itself, and a conclusion with a call to action that reinforces the purpose of the infographic. The story presents a beginning (introduction), middle (central message), and an end (conclusion). The substance of an infographic story also includes citing the sources of your information and visuals.

CRAFTING A CATCHY TITLE

The title is an infographic's best advertisement. It can sell or obscure an infographic in seconds. Therefore, the title should be relevant, engaging, and succinct. Unlike some titles of research and evaluation journal articles and dissertations, an infographic title should be catchy and draw the reader in. If you've ever attended a professional conference poster session, you know it's impossible to read every poster. As you peruse the gallery, you quickly scan titles for any that pique your interest. Think about how long you spend looking at any one title to determine if it could be relevant to you. Probably a couple seconds. The same could be said about posters and flyers in a subway station or on a bulletin board. Online, the competition for attention is endless, and it begins with the title.

The following are tips for crafting a catchy title:

- Speak to your audience. Use a language they understand.
- Be informative (Grant, 2013).
  - Pull inspiration from your central message. Think about the key takeaway for the infographic and use an apt title that fits in an interesting way.
  - Draw from your infographic's call to action. This reinforces how the infographic is intended to help or catalyze them.
  - Draw from the name of the program you've studied or its purpose.
- Keep it interesting (Paiva et al., 2012).
  - Use a play on words.
  - Use an allusion. Titles that allude to commonly known phrases, slogans, or references to pop culture, songs, or literary work can quickly capture attention (wikiHow, 2021).
- Look at other infographics for inspiration.
- Less is more. A shorter and captivating title will be easier to remember than a long and overly descriptive one (Grant, 2013; Subotic & Mukherjee, 2014).

FIGURE 3.1   ■   Infographic Example With Catchy Title

Source: Centers for Disease Control and Prevention and Prevention and Prevention, The More They Burn, the Better They Learn, 2010

The Center for Disease Control (CDC) uses infographics as a primary communication method for reaching its audiences. In the infographic below, they use a short, catchy title, *The More They Burn, the Better They Learn* (Figure 3.1). The two key words "burn" and "learn" not only rhyme, but also stand out with a different font color treatment. Both words represent the central message of the infographic—that is, students who are more physically active tend to earn higher academic grades. The title is also alluring because readers are left wondering who is "they," so they want to read more to find out. Less effective and catchy titles that you would avoid for this infographic would be, *Student Learning Is Associated With Physical Activity*, or *Win the Prize With Exercise*. The former reads like a statistical finding and the latter is catchy, but too vague and doesn't fully represent the point of the infographic.

SETTING THE SCENE WITH YOUR INTRODUCTION

The introduction lays the foundation for the central message and serves as a "hook" for the rest of the infographic. It communicates to the audience why they should care about the central message. For example, in the CDC infographic about physical activity and learning, the introductory hook is a simple question, "Did you know that kids who are physically active get better grades?" This question prepares the parent audience to absorb the research findings presented both visually and in text. This is an example of a simple introduction that primes the audience for the central message. Note that this infographic is pretty straightforward for a parent audience who might be more interested in the key implication of a research study than in the study data or methods. As such, the audience doesn't need more introductory information to understand the central message.

For infographics presenting more complex, comprehensive, or nuanced information, the introduction should include any important background or contextual information the audience needs to know to fully understand the central message of the infographic. This might include a statement about the problem the infographic addresses. For example, in the CDC's *Go Light When You Grab a Bite* infographic, the introduction includes a statement about the problem of leading busy lives and needing to buy meals on the go to save time (Figure 3.2). The introduction might also present statistics representing the problem the central message addresses. For example, an infographic about outcomes of a student reading program might use the introduction to present recent statistics about a decline in national student reading achievement. An infographic about preventative health practices involving hand washing might present increasing trends in the spread of infectious disease. By introducing the

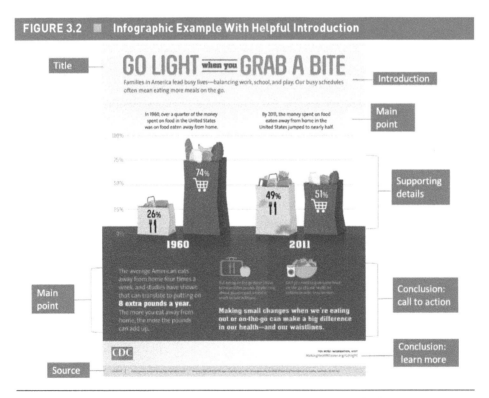

FIGURE 3.2   ■   Infographic Example With Helpful Introduction

Source: Centers for Disease Control and Prevention, Go Light When You Grab a Bite, 2009

problem at the beginning of the infographic, the audience will want to know more about the solution. This draws the reader into the story of your infographic and sets the foundation for your central message.

The following are considerations for setting the scene with the introduction:

- Keep it focused only on what the audience needs to know to understand the central message. It should not take away from your central message; avoid extraneous details.

- The length should be relatively short compared to the rest of the infographic.

- If appropriate, use a problem statement to help the reader understand the issue at hand and why they should care about it.

- Include any background information about the program that is the focus of the infographic. Briefly describing what the program offers, to whom, and when, provides the audience with context they might need to understand the central message.

DEVELOPING A COMPELLING CENTRAL MESSAGE

The core of the infographic is an organized presentation of information that communicates a memorable central message. It is the heart of the infographic's story. The central message is what you convey to your audience to achieve the infographic's purpose as discussed in Step 2. The central message may include main or secondary points as well as supporting details as needed. The central message emerges from information you already have, such as from a research or evaluation study. Working from the information and data you have, you determine the message worth sharing (Cairo, 2016).

There is no rule as to how many points—main or secondary—your infographic should include. Determining the points of your story will depend on the information you deem necessary to achieve your infographic's purpose and the hierarchy of that information. You might have multiple main points all sharing equal levels of importance and relevance to your central message. In the example infographic we created for a fictitious study of a reading program, iRead, we identified the purpose as increasing audience understanding of program outcomes (Figure 3.3). The infographic presents two key study findings: student engagement in reading and increased student reading achievement. These findings represent two main points in the infographic and hold equal importance. We also include secondary points about how student reading achievement changed over time and in comparison to students who did not participate in the iRead program. If this had been a real study and reading program, we would have considered the context of the study and the program's theory of change in designating findings as main or secondary in the infographic.

Regardless of how you organize the number and hierarchy of your points, they should all support the infographic's central message. In the iRead example, the central message would be students benefiting from participating in the reading program. The fewer points required to convey the central message, the better. Too many points can dilute the central message while also increasing the cognitive load on the audience to make sense of your message.

FIGURE 3.3   ■   Infographic Example With Multiple Main Points

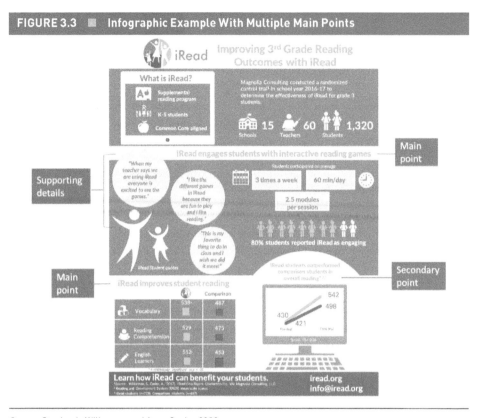

Source: Stephanie Wilkerson and Anne Cosby, 2022

The supporting details of your infographic's central message are your data points. These might include quantitative results, qualitative quotes, or other research findings that support the main and secondary points. For example, if a main point is that student reading achievement increased, the supporting detail would be that it increased by 23 points in one year. Quotes from interview or focus group data can bring to life main or secondary points in your infographic, such as in the iRead example (see Figure 3.3). You might also include other supporting details that explain or elaborate on a main or secondary point. For a main point about overall student reading achievement, a supporting detail could be that all students showed a significant increase in achievement regardless of gender, race/ethnicity, and socioeconomic status.

Deciding upon a hierarchy of information is important because it will guide the level of visual emphasis you want to give the information in your infographic. Generally, your infographic's main points along with supporting data points would have greater visual emphasis than the secondary points. You want to draw the audience's eye to the main points of the central message. In doing so, the hierarchy of information supports your infographic's purpose.

The CDC's *Go Light When You Grab a Bite* infographic could be interpreted as presenting two main points (see Figure 3.2). The first main point is that the money spent on food eaten away from the home has almost doubled. The supporting details for this main point are shown in the chart that presents the percentage change in spending for 1960 and 2011. The other main point is that the more you eat away from home, the more weight you are likely to gain. The supporting detail is that eating away from home four times a week resulted in gaining an extra eight pounds a year. The CDC might designate the points of this infographic differently based on how it assesses the importance and value of this information for its audience and the infographic's purpose.

Regardless of the number or levels of points, categorizing your infographic's central message into main and secondary points and supporting details is a critical step in organizing your thinking for an infographic. This is the process that will help you distill large, complex pieces of information into clearly defined chunks that the audience can understand and interpret.

The following are considerations for developing a compelling central message:

- Use as few points as necessary to communicate the infographic's central message.

- The more points you present, the more information your audience has to comprehend and recall.

- Consider how the points in the infographic relate to each other—are they of equal importance? Does one support the other? This will guide the relative visual emphasis in your infographic's design.

- Think of the data or evidence in your infographic as a supporting detail, not a main point. Your main point conveys what you want the reader to glean from the data or evidence.

CONCLUDING WITH PURPOSE

The conclusion closes the story by reinforcing the purpose of the infographic. In Step 2, you articulated a clear purpose for the infographic, framed as an intended outcome for the audience. Based on that purpose, consider what you want your audience to do with the information from the central message. Think of this as the "so what?" of your infographic. Your infographic presents a compelling message to your audience; now you conclude your story by showing the audience what is next. The conclusion tells readers what is most important to remember, what next steps to take, or where to learn more.

An infographic helps accomplish its purpose and empowers its audience when it includes a call to action. If the purpose of the infographic is to increase awareness or understanding, the conclusion might direct the audience to a website, report, or contact to learn more. It also might include a final statement that summarizes the infographic's main and secondary points into a key takeaway. If the purpose of the infographic is to change behavior, the conclusion might present actions audience members can take. For example, the conclusion in CDC's *Go Light When You Grab a Bite* infographic presents best practices to promote behavioral change, a call-to-action summary statement, and a link to learn more.

The following are considerations for concluding your infographic with purpose:

- Revisit your intended outcome for your infographic and the change you hope to catalyze in your audience.

- Reinforce the key takeaway from the main and secondary points of your central message.

- After reviewing the main points of your infographic, ask "so what?"—why does the information matter?

- The conclusion's call to action can be as simple as sharing where to go to learn more or as detailed as describing practices to change behavior.

CITING SOURCES

Like all research and evaluation reports, infographics should acknowledge the information sources clearly and directly. Your audience should be able to access and review the information sources for the infographic without having to search for them (Krum, 2014). If the infographic represents a full report, the report should be referenced with a hyperlink to it, if it lives online. If your infographic draws from other research findings, citations should be provided. For example, in CDC's *Go Light When You Grab a Bite* infographic, the very bottom references two sources from the literature that support the infographic's content (see Figure 3.2). Infographics will often use superscripts attached to a data visualization or statement with a corresponding URL address in this section of the infographic (Beegel, 2014). Sources for icons and images should be cited appropriately in this section of the infographic as well (see Step 4 for more information about determining if you need to seek permission or cite credit for an icon or image).

This section of the infographic might also include other technical or statistical information to validate or further support any data or findings you present in the infographic. This might include references to sample sizes (if not presented elsewhere), statistical values (p-values, effect sizes, coefficients), or data collection instruments, for example. Think of it as footnotes for the infographic. The font is smaller in size and therefore the section is minimized on the page. The information provided in this section is for readers who are interested in more technical details and sources of information for the infographic.

The infographic should also include your or your organization's information, such as logo, website address, or contact email. This is particularly important because infographics disseminate through online channels sometimes without any context or source information about its origin. You want to make sure the audience has access to all the information necessary should they want to learn more or cite the infographic in another publication. If you want to control how others will distribute, copy, or use the infographic, consider a licensing model, such as Creative Commons, for publishing your infographic with a copyright (Creative Commons, 2021). It is free of charge and allows you to specify the type of Creative Commons license that is most appropriate for how you want others to use the infographic.

The following are considerations for citing sources:

- Reference sources for data and research findings.
- Include statistical details that may not be integral to your infographic's story but are important to the credibility of your data.

- Include credits for any icons or images that require it.

- Include publishing information and copyright for your infographic.

BOX 3.1. STEP 3 DESIGN CHALLENGE
DESIGN CHALLENGE: WHAT IF THERE IS MORE INFORMATION FOR AN INFOGRAPHIC THAN WHAT CAN BE FEASIBLY INCLUDED IN A STORY?

When the information source for an infographic is a comprehensive research or evaluation report, the task of identifying only a few key points (main or secondary) to communicate your central message can feel daunting. If you are the study lead and report author, all the information included in your report might seem equally relevant and important for your audience. However, an infographic is not intended to supplant a report, *so what can you do when faced with the challenge of determining what to include in the infographic and what to leave out?*

Revisit the purpose and audience for your infographic. During Step 2, you identified the purpose of the infographic for the intended audience. This purpose serves as an anchor for deciding what information or data will help achieve the infographic's purpose. Determine the fewest number of key points that could accomplish the purpose of the infographic.

Refer your audience to source documents that provide more detail. Rather than attempting to overcrowd the infographic with too much information, include hyperlinks and references to source documents where your audience can learn more, if they are interested. This is an easy way to provide access to comprehensive information while honing your infographic's story to a few key points. This might be particularly appropriate for providing in-depth background information about the infographic's topic or elaborating on several study findings or data points.

Create a statement about your central message, purpose, and audience. Starting with an overall statement about your central message can be a useful tool before identifying your main and secondary points as well as supporting details. To create this statement, complete the sentence frame below with the information you created for Steps 1 and 2. When you read the sentence, it should make sense and distinguish between the purpose and the central message of your story. You might use this sentence to try out a few different ways to focus your infographic.

Create and compare a few storylines from beginning to end (title to conclusion). Developing different storylines allows you to consider different ways to accomplish your infographic's purpose. The central message for each storyline might be the same, but you also might discover there are multiple ways to convey it using different arrangements of main and secondary points and supporting details. This creative process can help you clarify your thinking and identify the key points that stand out in your story. When considering different storylines, be sure to refer back to what you know about the interests and information needs of your audience and the change you want to catalyze through your infographic.

BOX 3.2. PLANETS ILLUSTRATIVE EXAMPLE— CREATE THE STORY

In Step 2, we decided the purpose of the PLANETS infographic would be to increase STEM OST educators' understanding of the learner outcomes as a result of using the project's curriculum units. During Step 3, we created the story we would convey to OST educators to achieve the infographic's purpose. We narrowed our focus to learner outcomes, which directed us to review the main findings of the PLANETS evaluation study. In reviewing study findings, we knew that the PLANETS activities engage students in an engineering design process that involves collaborative problem-solving. We also knew this process was intended to build three habits of mind (i.e., negotiating designs collaboratively, persisting through failure, and celebrating success) and increase learner attitudes toward engineering. We decided to identify  these two learner outcomes (habits of mind and learner attitudes) as two main points of the story that support the infographic's purpose. Taken together, we determined the key message of the infographic's story would communicate that PLANETS activities build learners' habits of mind and improve their attitudes toward engineering by engaging them in collaborative problem-solving through an engineering design process. We put the first three steps—audience, purpose, story—together in a sentence frame to make sure it is clear (Table 3.1).

TABLE 3.1 ■ PLANETS Story Audience, Purpose, and Key Message	
Create the Story	
Step 1 **Audience**	STEM out-of-school time (OST) educators
Step 2 **Purpose**	To increase OST educators' understanding of the learner outcomes resulting from implementation of the PLANETS curricular units.
Step 3 **Key Message of the Story**	PLANETS activities build learners' habits of mind and improve their attitudes toward engineering by engaging them in collaborative problem solving through an engineering design process.

Put it together...

This infographic shares	that PLANETS activities build learners' habits of mind and improve their attitudes toward engineering
	(abridged key message)
with/for	STEM out-of-school time educators
	(audience)
in order to	increase their understanding of the learner outcomes resulting from implementation of the PLANETS curricular units.
	(purpose)

With the audience, purpose, and central message identified for the infographic's story, the next step was to draft the content. Using a graphic organizer, we brainstormed a title, introduction, main points, secondary points, supporting details, conclusion, and sources for the infographic (Table 3.2). Because we didn't yet know what the infographic would look like, we simply drafted ideas of information we thought would be important for communicating a clear and coherent story to the audience. We knew the content of the story would be revised and refined in later steps in the development process. We framed our main points as succinctly as possible as these would likely be header statements to include in the infographic. As such, we used the secondary points to give a more detailed description of what we meant by the statements for the main points. We identified OST educator perceptions as possible supporting details to reinforce the main and secondary points. However, we didn't yet know if we would include all details in the final story, but we wanted to document them in this step. Lastly, we drafted a simple conclusion and call to action to minimize wordiness, and we identified the citations and sources we knew we already needed to include, such as the details about the PLANETS project team, evaluation report, and a student survey used to collect student attitudinal data.

TABLE 3.2 ■ Draft Story Content for PLANETS

| Title | Think Like an Engineer, Act Like a Space Rover |
| | Where student minds meet real-world problems |

Introduction	● **What:** The Planetary Learning that Advances the Nexus of Engineering, Technology, and Science (PLANETS)[1] project provides out-of-school time (OST) educators with NASA planetary science content delivered through science and engineering activities. PLANETS middle school engineering guides, Testing the Waters: Engineering a Water Reuse Process (grades 6-8), Worlds Apart: Engineering Remote Sensing Devices (grades 6-8), and In Good Hands: Engineering Space Gloves (grades 3-5)
	● **Why:** PLANETS activities aim to build students' habits of mind and improve their attitudes toward engineering by engaging them in collaborative problem solving through an engineering design process.
	● **Who:** Study participants included 15 OST sites, 215 youth, and 18 educators

Main Points	Secondary Points	Supporting Details
1. Students demonstrated three habits of mind practices that enhance student attitudes toward engineering.[2]	1. Negotiating designs collaboratively: working together to design a solution to the given engineering challenge 2. Persisting through failure: evaluating what went wrong in a design, and planning for improvement 3. Celebrating successes: when a design improvement results in a positive outcome.	Educator quote: "It really started with the learners wanting it to be solved—and then they started to persist."

2. Middle school youth showed statistically significant increases in positive attitudes toward engineering as a result of their participation. [3]	Increases in student attitudes were evident for items such as <ul><li>"Engineering is useful in helping to solve the problems of everyday life" (Value to Society)</li><li>"Engineering helps me understand today's world" (Value to Me)</li><li>"We learn about important things when we do engineering in school" (School)</li><li>"I am interested when we do engineering in school" (Enjoyment)</li><li>"I really want to learn engineering" (Aspirations)</li></ul>	As a result of participating in PLANETS, educators perceived that students gained a deeper understanding of the engineering design process, learned about science careers, were engaged in the activities, and more interested in science and engineering.

Conclusion or Call to Action	Use of engineering curricula that emphasize the engineering design process can shape youth habits of mind and increase their attitudes toward STEM. Access the PLANETS materials for use in your out-of-school time setting. Links to PLANETS website: planets-stem.org
Sources (references)	[1] NASA 5-year grant involving a collaborative partnership with the Center for Science Teaching and Learning (CSTL) at Northern Arizona University (NAU), the U.S. Geological Survey (USGS) Astrogeology Science Center, and the Museum of Science, Boston (MOS) [2] Lachapelle, C.P. & Brennan, R.T. (2018). An instrument for examining elementary engineering student interests and attitudes. *International Journal of Education in Mathematics, Science and Technology (IJEMST)*, 6(3), 221–240. DOI: 10.18404/ijemst.428171 https://www.ijemst.net/index.php/ijemst/article/view/289 [3] Haden, C. & Peery, E. (2021). Evaluation of the NASA-Funded Planetary Learning that Advances the Nexus of Engineering, Technology, and Science (PLANETS) Project: Five-Year Summative Evaluation Report. Charlottesville, VA: Magnolia Consulting. [Note: If publicly available, add link to full report in the infographic] Creative Commons license

NOW IT'S YOUR TURN!

- Find an infographic online and see if you can determine what the central message, main points, secondary points, and supporting details are (for example, Visme's best infographic examples at https://visme.co/blog/best-infographic-examples/). Can you find infographics with a call to action as a conclusion? Do the infographics cite sources or refer to Creative Commons?

- Create your content: Using the table below, draft the key elements of your story including the title; introduction; main points, secondary points, and supporting details; conclusion; and sources (Table 3.3). When complete, review it to ensure every point and detail supports your infographic's purpose for the intended audience. Remove any points or details that do not align with the purpose of your infographic or support the coherence of your story's central message.

TABLE 3.3 ■ Graphic Organizer for Infographic Story Content

	Main Points	Secondary Points	Supporting Details
Title			
Introduction			
Conclusion or Call to Action			
Sources (references)			

RESOURCES

Check it out!

- Nancy Duarte's Big Idea and 3-Minute Story in *Resonate* (2010).

- Cole Nussbaumer Knaflic's Storytelling With data: A Data Visualization Guide for Business Professionals (2015).

- Exercise for creating titles adapted from Richard Leahy's "Twenty Titles for the Writer." http://writing.umn.edu/sws/assets/pdf/quicktips/titles.pdf

STEP 4: IDENTIFY DATA AND VISUALS

LEARNING OBJECTIVES

In Step 4, you will learn how to

- identify what data you need to support your infographic's story,

- decide which visuals will best represent your data and the content of your story,

- select culturally sensitive visuals that are appropriate for your infographic's audience, and

- determine if you need permission to use the visuals for your infographic.

The infographic development process begins with crafting a powerful message in Steps 1 through 3 by identifying your audience, clarifying the infographic's purpose, and creating the story that conveys the infographic's central message. These three steps lay the foundation for bringing your infographic's story to life. Next, the development process moves into the design phase of infographic production through Steps 4 through 7. As part of developing a visual story, you will identify the data and visuals for the infographic (Step 4), select an appropriate layout (Step 5), choose design elements (Step 6), and sketch ideas (Step 7). These steps prepare a blueprint for drafting the infographic in Step 8.

If you can look at an infographic and understand its message with minimal supporting text, your visuals are "showing" the story. While text may provide explanation and supporting details, an effective infographic is able to convey the story without fully relying on the text. The more text on the page, the more time and mental processing is required for your audience to understand the central message. When you design your infographic as if you have the audience's attention for only three minutes, you want your visuals to represent your central message so the audience can quickly understand and remember it (Medina, 2014; Solso, 2003; Zull, 2002). By leveraging the power of visual communication, you can capture your audience's attention, engage them in the story, and accomplish your infographic's purpose (Djamasbi et al., 2010; Dunlap & Lowenthal, 2016).

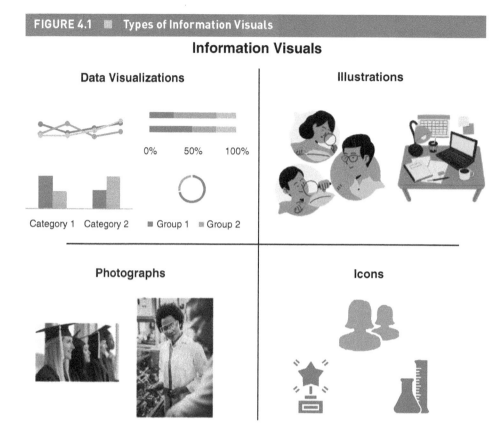

FIGURE 4.1 ■ **Types of Information Visuals**

In Step 4, you identify the visual elements that will "show" and communicate your infographic's story efficiently and effectively. Visual elements can include icons, photographs, illustrations, and data displays (Figure 4.1). They can be static, clickable (e.g., screen tips and popup boxes), animated (e.g., gifs), and interactive (e.g., click to view information different ways). Selecting visuals to show your story is an intentional process that begins by revisiting the story elements from Step 3 and determining which elements are central to communicating the central message. Once you identify what information you want to present, then you determine how to visually present it. This might be an iterative process as you discover how well the visuals you select are ones that you can feasibly develop or access, tell a visual story sufficiently, and are culturally appropriate for your audience.

IDENTIFYING DATA FOR YOUR INFOGRAPHIC

A compelling infographic story is backed by data that gives credibility to the central message. To identify what data you might use in an infographic, refer to the story elements you crafted during Step 3, including introductory information, main points, supporting details, and the conclusion. As you review each story element, consider what data you already have, such as from a research or evaluation report, and what data you might need to find or collect. Visuals should represent data truthfully and accurately. Data should not be taken out of context or distorted to communicate a story that is contrary to the original information source.

The 10-step infographic development process doesn't begin with identifying data and visuals. It starts with identifying your audience, purpose, and message, and *then* determining what data you need to support the story. This is particularly helpful if you have a large amount of data because it helps you identify the data most pertinent to the central message. If you are working from a research or evaluation report, for example, you might have a plethora of data and findings to consider for an infographic. The data or visuals presented in the report, however, shouldn't drive infographic development, rather the infographic's purpose and message should.

There is no rule of thumb as to how much data you need to present in an infographic or for what story elements you need to present it. Minimally, the main point of your story should have data backing it to convey its credibility. Audiences want information they can trust, and reliable data is one way to represent the integrity of an infographic. Data might include qualitative or quantitative information, depending on your audience and what types of data will be credible to them. Sometimes including both types of data, for example quotes and survey ratings, provides complementary evidence supporting your message. However, consider how much data is necessary to communicate your message, while being mindful of how much data your audience will fully process and remember in a matter of minutes. Oversaturating your infographic with data could lessen the clarity and impact of your central message as it might be difficult for readers to discern which data is most relevant. The less data you need to communicate your message, the less cognitive burden you place on your audience. "Less is more" when you want the audience to remember data that communicates the main point of your story (Veletsianos, 2010).

In addition to the main point, you might consider other story elements that could be communicated with data to support the infographic's central message. For example, some infographics present a problem statement as part of the introduction for the visual story. The *Midwives for Haiti* infographic (Figure 4.2) sets the stage for the visual story by presenting data that represents the severity of the problem the program aims to solve—that is, maternal and infant mortality. The infographic also uses data to communicate its main points about how the program reduces maternal and infant mortality. Given the amount of information included in this infographic, the introductory background information about the problem would be obscured if presented as text only, and the significance of the program's purpose and impact would be less compelling. When choosing which story elements to represent with data, consider how each data point contributes to communicating the infographic's central message.

Not all information presented in an infographic will have a data source. Examples of information that might not need a data source include introductory background information that presents a program description, supporting details that elaborate on a main point, a conclusion that reiterates the central message, or a call to action that reinforces the infographic's purpose. While this type of information might not need a data source, it can still be represented visually to show the infographic's story.

FIGURE 4.2 ▓ Example of Introductory Information Describing a Problem

2013 ANNUAL REPORT

The Problem

Maternal Mortality Rate in Haiti

350 Deaths | **100,000** Births

US Rate is

12.7 Deaths

100,000 Births

7%

of children die before age five.

That is 1 in every 14 children.

Lifetime risk of maternal death **1 | 83**

Among the poorest quintile (1/5) of women have **6%** skilled care

94% are cared for by Matrons or family members

75% of women do not have a skilled attendant at delivery

ESTIMATED NUMBER OF SKILLED BIRTH ATTENDANTS NEEDED TO REDUCE MATERNAL MORTALITY BY 75% IN HAITI AND ACHIEVE MILLENIUM DEVELOPMENT GOAL 5:

563

So, we train Haitian nurses to become Skilled Birth Attendants.

Source: UNICEF

We deliver high impact projects to reduce maternal and infant mortality in Haiti. By working collaboratively with Haitian organizations to determine the most culturally appropriate methods, we achieve lasting change for our graduates and the mothers and children they serve.

| 243000 |
| 166402 |

0   50000   150000   250000   350000

■ Grants ■ 2012 Surplus ■ Private Donations
2013 Revenue: $697,768

■ Haiti Programs (86%) ■ Administrative Costs (14%)
2013 Expenses: $657,724

21 ← NUMBER OF SKILLED BIRTH ATTENDANTS TRAINED IN 2013

NUMBER OF SKILLED BIRTH → **75** ATTENDANTS TRAINED SINCE 2006

HIGH IMPACT PROJECTS

2,143 births attended by our midwives and students at St. Therese Hospital

$4000 funds the education and training of each student

$3600 funds salary of midwife

32 Traditional Birth Attendants trained in Matron Outreach Program

$1500 funds matron training

5,607 maternal care visits at Mobile Prenatal Clinic

$19,920 funds annual supplies to 16 rural villages

$10,800 funds the salaries of 3 clinic midwives

Special thanks to our 95 volunteers, 924 donors and the continued support of Every Mother Counts, Phalen Family Foundation, SG Foundation, Virginia Women's Center and Bon Secours Health System.

To sponsor a midwife or rural clinic, volunteer your skills, become a partner or corporate sponsor, or to make a tax-deductible donation please visit: **www.midwivesforhaiti.org**

Source: Midwives for Haiti, 2013

IDENTIFYING VISUALS THAT SHOW YOUR INFOGRAPHIC'S STORY

Once you determine what data you will use for your infographic, you can identify what visual elements will represent those data and other information to show your infographic's story. The visual elements in an infographic will draw the audience in and help them understand the story's central message. The visuals should be purposeful and relevant to the story, rather than extraneous or decorative. The goal of this step is to select or develop visuals that help communicate the story.

To identify the visual elements for your story, refer to the data you identified at the beginning of Step 4 and the content you generated in Step 3 for your infographic (i.e., title, introduction, main and secondary points, supporting details, and conclusion or call to action). Highlight key words, data points, or ideas from your data and story components that are germane to the infographic's central message. Consider the subject of your infographic, such as an individual or group of individuals, content or programmatic focus, or a data point or study finding tied to a main point of your infographic's story. When thinking about study findings, note what the finding represents, such as differences between things, relationships among things, improvement, frequency, etc., as this would be what you want to show visually. Next, brainstorm possible visualizations for these aspects of the infographic, keeping in mind this is an exploratory phase of development and your visualizations will evolve over time.

For example, the *America Land of Corn* infographic by Suzanne Boretz and Allison Agoff uses a flow diagram, icons, illustrations, and bar graphs to describe the corn industry and corn's different uses (Figure 4.3). The flow diagram splits into five branches showing the distribution outlets for corn produced in the United States. The thickness of each branch represents the percentage of corn going to each distribution outlet. For example, the branch representing the 39% of corn production going to animal feed is much thicker than the 8% exported to other countries. This visual makes it easy for the reader to see the proportion of corn production allocated across its primary uses. For each of the five areas branching from the flow diagram, the infographic communicates supporting details with icons, icon arrays, icon graphs, and bar graphs. Through these depictions, the infographic visually communicates a large amount of information in easily digestible and interpretable chunks. This example also illustrates how visuals can show several points of an infographic story with minimal supporting text.

Identifying appropriate visuals to represent data and story content can be one of the most challenging aspects of creating an infographic. Icons, for example, can serve many uses in infographics including representing concrete things (e.g., swimming, horse, tree), abstract things (e.g., questioning, care, accomplishment), and quantities (e.g., percentage or amount of something; Figure 4.4). Icon arrays and icon graphs are also common ways to represent quantities (see Figure 4.4).

You also want to be mindful of gender representation when using people-like icons in your infographic and ensure the icons you use represent your audience. Noun Project and other icon websites include a variety of icons that are gender neutral and transgender (Figure 4.5). The type of icon used in icon arrays can affect mental processing of information and memory recall

FIGURE 4.3 ■ Example of Visuals Showing the Story

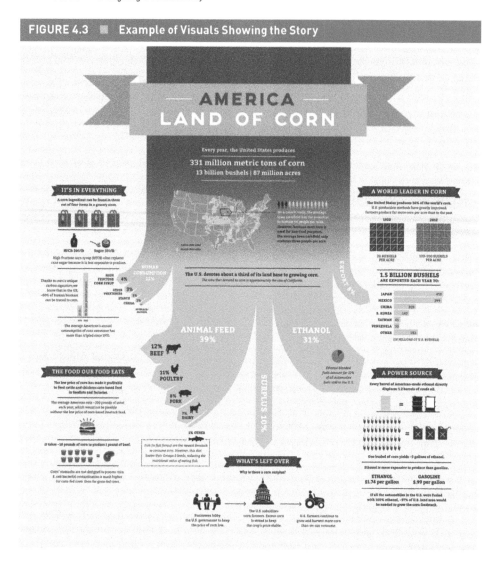

because readers typically relate to people-like icons more than circles or other shapes used in an array (Zikmund-Fisher et al., 2014). Therefore, using appropriate people-like icons for your intended audience will promote more efficient information uptake, comprehension, and recall.

This is an opportune time to search online for ideas and inspiration on websites for icons (e.g., Noun Project), stock photos (e.g., iStock), data visualization galleries (e.g., Data Viz Project), and specific content or programs (e.g., Google image search using key terms from your infographic story). If your infographic is for a program you are researching or evaluating, visit the program's website to see what visuals they use and might be available to you. Do not purchase or commit to any visual elements at this point. During this step, you are exploring and documenting possibilities.

FIGURE 4.4   ▨   **Icon Representations in Infographics**

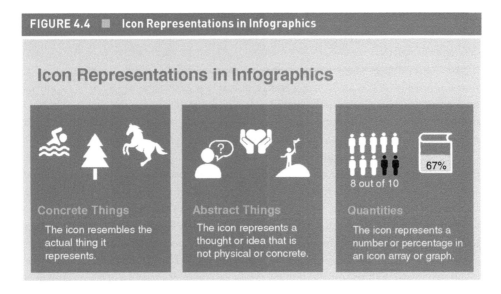

FIGURE 4.4   ▨   **Icon Representations in Infographics**

FIGURE 4.5   ▨   **Gender Neutral and Transgender Icons**

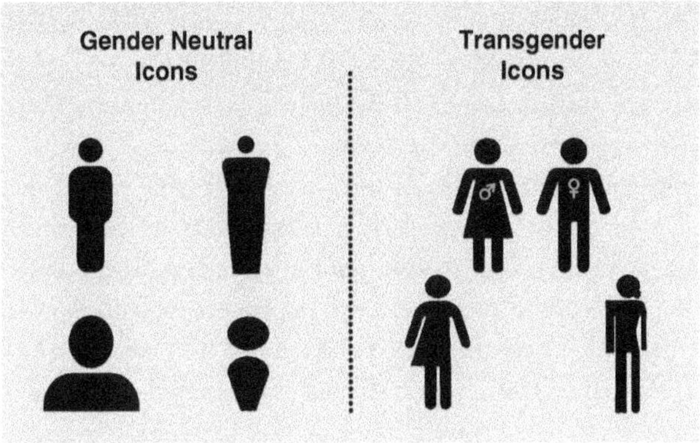

You might consider multiple visual options for representing a key word, data point, or idea for your story. For example, in the *Midwives for Haiti* example, the infographic represents a midwife using a photograph and a nurse icon (see Figure 4.2). Each visual element represents a midwife for two story components and for slightly different purposes. The photograph serves as a focal point in the title to make a human connection and draw the audience in, whereas the nurse icon provides programmatic background information about training nurses to serve as midwives. Because images of people convey social presence, they can positively affect the overall visual appeal of an infographic (Faraday, 2000). Therefore, if your infographic focuses on particular individuals, including a photograph may strengthen the appeal of your infographic's story. By identifying multiple ways to visually represent the same concept, you have more options to consider when you move to the design phase later in the development process.

You might already have a data visualization, such as a chart or graph, you want to use for your infographic. If you are working from a research or evaluation report, it is a common tendency to create an infographic around a data visualization from your report. Although this might save time and create continuity between your infographic and report, try to avoid using a single data visualization as the starting point for developing your infographic. Data visualizations, when done well, tell a story and make a clear point. They might exist in a full-length report, which also tells a larger story and makes several points. Uprooting an extant data visualization from one context and planting it into an infographic context assumes that the stories for the two are the same. Sometimes that is the case, but it's best not to arrive at that determination by starting infographic development with a data visualization. Begin instead by establishing your infographic's audience, purpose, and story, and *then* determine if an extant data visualization represents what your infographic needs to communicate visually. Failing to do so could result in an infographic that has an attractive focal point that grabs the audience's attention, but fails to communicate a clear and powerful message that they will remember.

The type of data visualization you use (e.g., line graph, bar chart, or icon display) should be appropriate for the data it represents and the point it is to convey. Your audience should be able to interpret the data visualization with ease and connect it to the overall story of the infographic. While this book does not delve into data visualization best practices, there are plenty of resources to guide you, such as Stephanie Evergreen's books, *Effective Data Visualization* and *Presenting Data Effectively* (see resource list at end of chapter).

When selecting or developing visuals for your infographic, also consider their relative importance to each other and the overall story. Is there a visual that best communicates the message? Is there a sequencing or a hierarchy of importance among them? Understanding the relationship among the visuals of the infographic will inform how you display them in later steps of the development process. For example, main points should be represented by larger visuals with one serving as the infographic's focal point (see more on focal points in Step 6). The focal point is what the eye gravitates to when you first look at an infographic (Atchison & Smith, 2000). You want to use the focal point to draw attention to a main point of your infographic story. Secondary points and supporting details can be captured in smaller visuals. During Step 4, you identify relevant and appropriate visuals and consider how together they will communicate the infographic's story.

The following are considerations for identifying visuals for your infographic:

- Visuals should be simple, clear, and easy to understand. They should be free of clutter and anything that would distract your audience or increase cognitive burden (Evergreen, 2017).

- Use visuals that represent pertinent information to convey your point. Avoid sidetracking the audience with unnecessary details that are interesting but not germane to the story (Knaflic, 2015).

- When selecting or developing visualizations, consider what will engage and make sense to your audience (Kirk, 2019). Overly elaborate or statistically complex visualizations could disengage your audience.

- Ensure visuals represent data and study findings truthfully and accurately. Do not manipulate data visualizations in a way that could result in interpreting the meaning differently from the original data source (Cairo, 2016).

- Consider how the visuals you have selected or developed relate to each other and their relative role in showing your infographic's story (Evergreen, 2018).

USING CULTURALLY SENSITIVE VISUALS

Because visuals have the power to draw the audience into your infographic without them reading accompanying text, it is important to use culturally sensitive visuals that accurately communicate your message for the intended audience (St. Amant, 2015; Veletsianos, 2010). As Randy Krum (2014, p. 19) states in his book, *Cool Infographics*, "All data visualization is biased." Despite methodological and statistical processes to minimize data bias, whenever you make a choice about what information and data to include in an infographic, what not to include, and how to represent it, there is the potential for bias in the decision-making process. You are likely selecting data and visuals based on your preferences, expertise, experience, and perspective related to the infographic's focus and story (Devine, 1989). These are things you might take for granted because they may be deeply ingrained in your professional practice and culture, which may be different from that of your audience. Engage in a self-examination and exploration of your own cultural and professional background, beliefs, and values, and consider how they might influence what data and visual elements you use in the infographic. Invite feedback from people who represent the infographic's audience to improve your cultural awareness and understanding of how others might interpret the infographic's visuals. Therefore, in selecting or developing visuals, be aware of your cultural assumptions because what you believe a visual represents to you, might not represent the same thing to your audience (St. Amant, 2015).

When selecting visuals, avoid using visual representations of outdated, negative, inappropriate, or oversimplified stereotypes related to gender, race, religion, disability, age, social class, profession, or country of origin (Burgio & Moretti, 2017; Pickens, 1982). For example, you would not use a photo of a woman in a short business skirt to portray a classroom teacher, nor would your infographic include images of only White women to represent the teaching field. Instead, you would want to depict a more realistic presentation of the teaching field that includes a range of culturally diverse teachers based on gender, race, and age who are dressed more realistically as teachers, rather than corporate business employees. Full diverse representation might not be struck in each visual, but you can achieve balance across the totality of visuals in the infographic in order to convey the infographic's message with cultural sensitivity (Burgio & Moretti, 2017).

You will also want to consider how your audience might interpret and understand visual symbols, such as icons, in your infographic based on their cultural background. For example, a thumbs-up icon might convey approval or a job well done in the United States and many other countries. However, in the Middle East, Australia, and Greece, for example, the thumbs-up symbol has a negative and insulting connotation, much the same way a raised middle finger has the United States. Because symbols can have multiple meanings and interpretations, you might select a few options to consider for your infographic at this stage of development. Getting feedback from representatives of your audience will help you determine which option they will most accurately interpret.

The infographic, *Physical Activity for Adults With Disabilities*, captures the cultural context of its audience, South African adults with disabilities (Figure 4.6). The infographic authors followed World Health Organization guidelines to ensure content accuracy and included South African adults with disabilities on the development team to create a culturally appropriate infographic (Naidoo et al., 2022). The inclusive team selected terms and phrasing that would be socially acceptable among adults with disabilities, starting with the title. The team agreed on using colors representing the South African flag (i.e., red, blue, green, and black with white borders) to make the infographic more culturally relevant. Visuals needed to be appropriate both for adults with disabilities and the South African context. For example, showing an image of a person getting dressed to represent a task that physical activity can make easier is relatable for a person with disabilities. A person in a wheelchair lifting weights shows an appropriate form of physical activity that a person with disabilities might do. Conversely, the team chose not to include swimming as an activity because many people in South Africa have a fear of swimming. While a thumbs-up symbol has a negative connotation is some countries, the team selected it for this infographic to represent improving mental health and quality of life in South Africa. As another culturally relevant symbol, the team chose an image of a South African handshake because it represents a customary greeting when meeting new people.

The following are considerations for using culturally sensitive visuals in your infographic:

- Step back to examine what cultural assumptions you might be making when selecting or developing visuals for the infographic.

- Solicit input from representatives of your audience to learn if they interpret and understand the meaning of the visuals the way you intend.

- When you search online for an image, use search terms that include words such as "diverse" or terms that specify cultural characteristics you want to represent.

- Look for and use filter options on online stock photo or image sites to select for ethnicity, for example.

FIGURE 4.6 ■ Example of a Culturally Sensitive Infographic

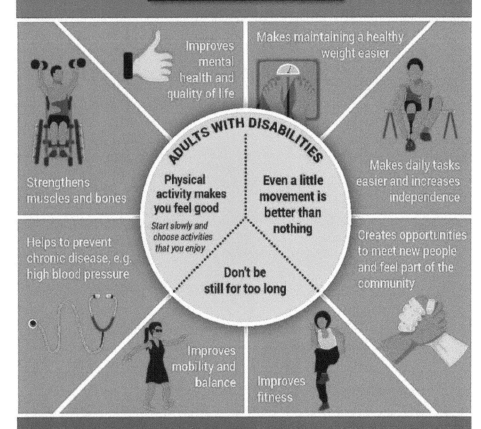

Physical Activity for Adults with Disabilities

Make it a daily habit

Improves mental health and quality of life

Makes maintaining a healthy weight easier

ADULTS WITH DISABILITIES

Physical activity makes you feel good

Start slowly and choose activities that you enjoy

Even a little movement is better than nothing

Makes daily tasks easier and increases independence

Strengthens muscles and bones

Don't be still for too long

Helps to prevent chronic disease, e.g. high blood pressure

Creates opportunities to meet new people and feel part of the community

Improves mobility and balance

Improves fitness

Include strength and balance activities on at least two days per week

For best health gains aim for 150 minutes each week of moderate intensity activity

 Moderate intensity activity increases your heart rate and makes you 'huff and puff'

  Adapted from the UK Chief Medical Officer's Guidelines 2011

DETERMINING LICENSING REQUIREMENTS FOR VISUALS

In selecting visuals for the infographic, you need to know if they are protected by copyright or considered public domain. If they are public domain, then the visuals are free to use without any licensing agreement or fee. While it might seem ideal, often visual choices can be limiting. If the visuals you want to use in your infographic are copyrighted, then you will need to understand the licensing agreement for them. This includes any requirements around citing the author, artist, or source of the image. Usage rights also stipulate if you can use the visuals for commercial purposes in which you would make money from their use, or for editorial use in which you can't modify the image. Typically visuals for research and evaluation purposes require neither commercial use nor editorial rights. Licensing agreements will also specify if you have to provide attribution to the original creator of the work. If attribution is required, review the agreement to determine how to credit the visual, such as through providing the creator's name, link to website, or other type of mention.

Another type of copyright license to be aware of are Creative Commons licenses. Creative Commons copyright licenses provide a standardized way to indicate what type of copyright permissions are granted for creative work. A licensor can specify what type of Creative Commons license to use for their work and whether or not to allow others to distribute, copy, or use their work commercially (Creative Commons, 2021). For example, many free icons on the Noun Project website are licensed under Creative Commons and require that you give credit to the creator or purchase a royalty-free license.

Stock image websites (e.g., iStock, Unsplash, Pixabay) typically use royalty-free licenses where you pay one time to use a copyrighted visual for creative use, whether that is personal or commercial. Once an image has been purchased, you are able to use and modify visuals for your infographic without needing to cite attribution to the original creator.

The following are licensing considerations for visuals:

- Determine if the visual is copyrighted or in the public domain; the latter is free and does not require attribution.

- A royalty-free license involves making a one-time payment so you can use and modify an image without attribution.

- Always provide attribution to the original creator of copyrighted work when the licensing agreements requires it.

- Check the license required for every visual that you plan to use for your infographic. Websites offering visuals such as photos and icons typically have a license FAQ page that will provide guidance on what attribution, if any, needs to be given. License requirements may vary by website.

BOX 4.1. STEP 4 DESIGN CHALLENGE

DESIGN CHALLENGE: HOW DO I KNOW IF I HAVE THE RIGHT NUMBER AND TYPES OF VISUAL ELEMENTS?

In the process of identifying visual elements for an infographic, you will find yourself perusing numerous sources for ideas, inspiration, and image collection. When the visual possibilities for your infographic seem limitless, you might accrue several options for your infographic. This could result in a collection of different types of photographs, icons, images, illustrations, and data displays to represent aspects of your infographic story. At this point in the development process, *what can you do when faced with the challenge of determining if you have the right number and types of visuals?*

Review your visuals as a collection, not just individually. When you look at your visual elements together, check to see if they show a coherent story. Ensure each one does its part to represent an aspect of your infographic's story. See if they fit together as a collection to represent your story. If there are any outliers that don't contribute to the story, remove them and see if the visual story still maintains itself without them.

Make sure your visuals complement, rather than compete with each other. You should arrive at a harmonious collection of visuals for your infographic. You might not fully discern if they are harmonious until you see them in a draft layout, but you should be able to see if they might compete for visual attention. Too many bold photographs and complex data displays, for example, could distract the reader's attention and make it more difficult to discern which is most important to the overall message.

Include some variation in types of visuals. An infographic that has only one type of visual, such as photographs or charts, might not "show" a compelling or engaging story. Using a variety of visual elements, that are coherent and complementary, can make for a more appealing visual story.

BOX 4.2. PLANETS ILLUSTRATIVE EXAMPLE— IDENTIFY DATA AND VISUALS

In Step 3, we fleshed out the content for the PLANETS infographic. Now in Step 4 we determine what data will support the infographic's content and what visuals will best represent the data and other information we want to include. For each story element—title, introduction, main points, conclusion, and sources—we considered what data we might need. Based on the content for the title, conclusion, and sources, we determined we would not need any data. We referred to the PLANETS evaluation report to identify what data were available to support information for the introduction as well as the infographic's two main points. Based on this review, we determined we had sufficient data to support the content of the PLANETS infographic story.

Working from the data and other content we identified for the story, we brainstormed visual ideas for the infographic, including key words, concepts, and study findings that supported the infographic's main points (Figure 4.7). To generate ideas, we searched imagery in the PLANETS curriculum units, NASA's Science Activation program materials, and NASA's online Scientific Visualization Studio. Using these sources, we found a couple versions of the PLANETS logo for consideration, a snapshot of the PLANETS curriculum units, and an image of the PLANETS mascot, "Rosie," who represents the Mars rover. We also viewed a variety of space imagery we thought we might use for different parts the infographic. We made sure to document any credits and permissions we would need if we used any of the images we selected as options, and also noted that they would be considered public domain, and therefore, free to use. For key words such as educators, learners, and habits of mind, we searched the Noun Project website for possible icons. To visualize one of the infographic's main points about the increase in student attitudes, we excerpted a couple bar charts based on OST learner and educator surveys from the PLANETS evaluation report.

In reviewing our considerations for visual images, we found them to be culturally appropriate for the OST educator audience. We also thought there was an appropriate balance among icons, photos, and data displays. We did not know during this step in the development process if we would use all the data or visuals in the final infographic—that would occur during subsequent steps that focus on the size, layout, and visual organization of the content on the page. We believed, however, that we had a good starting point and sufficient imagery for communicating a visual story.

TABLE 4.1 ■ PLANETS Data and Visuals for Infographic Story Elements				
Infographic Content	What data do you have or need to support the content?	What visuals would best represent your data and content? List key words, concepts, or images that will visually communicate your message. (e.g., graph, chart, icon, photo, illustration)	Is it culturally appropriate for the audience?	Do I need permission to use these visuals?
Title				
Introduction				
Main Point 1 (including any secondary points and supporting details)				
Main Point 2 (including any secondary points and supporting details)				

NOW IT'S YOUR TURN!

- Find an infographic online and see if the visuals "show" a culturally sensitive story (for example, visit Venngage's article on 8 Best Practices for Designing Infographics for Diversity and Inclusion: https://venngage.com/blog/designing-for-diversity/).
  - In what ways is the infographic culturally sensitive?
  - What draws your eye when you look at the infographic? That is the focal point. Does it represent a main point?
  - If you only look at the visuals, can you glean the infographic's story or central message?
  - Are the visuals easy to interpret, or is what they represent unclear? How would you change them to be more culturally sensitive?

TABLE 4.2 ■ Identifying Data and Visuals for Infographic Story Elements				
Infographic Content	What data do you have or need to support the content?	What visuals would best represent your data and content? List key words, concepts, or images that will visually communicate your message (e.g., graph, chart, icon, photo, illustration).	Is it culturally appropriate for the audience?	Do I need permission to use these visuals?
Title				
Introduction				
Main Point 1 (including any secondary points and supporting details)				
Main Point 2 (including any secondary points and supporting details)				
Conclusion or Call to Action				

- Do all visual elements support the central message, or are there any that are distracting and extraneous? Are there any visuals that could be removed from the infographic and not change the central message?

- Identify your visuals. Using Table 4.2 above, identify any data you have or might need to support the content of each story element (title, introduction, main points, secondary points, and supporting details; conclusion; and sources; Table 4.2). You might only have one main point to your story. Remember, how you structure the points will depend on the hierarchical nature of the information you present in the infographic.

RESOURCES

Check it out!

- Alberto Cairo's The Truthful Art: Data, Charts, and Maps for Communication (2016).

- Stephanie Evergreen's Effective Data Visualization: The Right Chart for the Right Data (2017) and Presenting Data Effectively: Communicating Your Findings for Maximum Impact (2018).

- Andy Kirk's Data Visualization: A Handbook for Data Driven Design (2019).

- Judy E. Pickens' Without Bias: A Guidebook for Nondiscriminatory Communication (1982).

- Diverse icons and fonts: https://venngage.com/blog/march-update-new-icons-new-fonts/

- Noun Project: https://thenounproject

STEP 5: SELECT A LAYOUT

LEARNING OBJECTIVES

In Step 5, you will learn how to

- plan an infographic layout that accounts for how your audience will interface with it,

- select a layout that supports the nature of the infographic's story, and

- create balance in your layout by using design rules and white space.

By this point in the infographic development process, you have created a compelling message with a clear purpose for an intended audience. You have identified visual information, including data, icons, and images, that will "show" the infographic's story. But a powerful infographic is not a random assortment of attractive visuals, data, and findings thrown onto a page haphazardly or without careful thought. A powerful infographic has an intentional layout designed to help accomplish the infographic's purpose by presenting a clear and well-organized story.

In Step 1, you determined if your audience would access the infographic through a report, social media, or website, for example, and whether your audience might view it in a printable or digital format. We consider accessibility and format of the infographic because they inform the appropriate size for your infographic's layout. In Step 5, you will also consider the nature of the infographic's story as a driver for how you organize visual information on the page. Different layouts might be suitable if you are presenting information hierarchically, categorically, comparatively, sequentially, or descriptively. Finally, you will need to think about your layout's balance and how it will flow and be organized to direct the reader's focus to the story's central message through different sections and use of white space.

LAYOUT AND AUDIENCE INTERFACE

Knowing if your audience will view the infographic in a print or digital format and in a vertical or horizontal orientation will dictate almost every other layout consideration. This informs size restrictions associated with each format and how you will organize information on the page.

By designing an infographic in the same size and orientation for how audiences will interface with it, you ensure consistency and transferability of your content. If you design an infographic in a size longer or wider than the actual size in which audiences will view it, you risk distorting the content and throwing off the infographic's design when you transfer it from your design program to its format for dissemination in Step 10. Determining size and orientation during this phase of development will prevent any need to resize, reformat, or rewrite your infographic's contents later in the process and will save you time in the long run. In Step 5, we are considering how size and orientation, in general, influence the layout and organization of information on the page. In Step 8, we discuss how to set the size parameters for your infographic based on the program you use to develop it and where the infographic will live.

Print Versus Digital Formats

Print and digital formats have unique layout opportunities and challenges. Print-friendly infographics provide audiences with flexibility for reading, notating, saving, and accessing without Internet connectivity. Research suggests that we comprehend and remember more when we read something in a printed format compared to a digital format (Clinton, 2019). Infographics designed for printing should fit on a single piece of paper where all text and visuals are legible. This naturally creates size constraints for the infographic's layout, including limits on the size and number of sections, visualizations, and text you can include in your infographic. For example, if the infographic will be printed or embedded in a report or other document, then you would set the size of the infographic in the design program to letter size (8 1/2 x 11") in the United States and A4 (210 x 297 mm) in Europe.[1] If embedded in a report, you will want to account for the document's margins as they will further limit the amount of space you have for the infographic content. Note, if working with an online template, the free account might not allow for resizing the infographic, so you will want to check the infographic size of a free account as it might not be conducive to printing letter size.

BOX 5.1. COMMON SOCIAL MEDIA IMAGE SIZES

Different social media sites have different image requirements for posts:

- Twitter: 1600 x 900 pixels
- Facebook: 1200 x 630 pixels
- LinkedIn: 1200 x 627 pixels

Many online sites with infographic templates have a function that allows for resizing your infographic to a preset size for specific social media platforms. While this will automatically rescale your infographic, aspects of your design could still be compromised. Note, the resizing feature may require a paid account.

For more details visit:

https://blog.hootsuite.com/social-media-image-sizes-guide/

While digital infographics that live online promote information accessibility and dissemination, different Internet browsers may impact how your infographic looks, and it can be challenging to ensure a consistent viewing experience between web and mobile viewing. Additionally, it is important to keep your infographic's size in mind when considering how readers will access and view the infographic online. For example, if your intention is for the audience to read the full infographic on different social media platforms, it is important to size your infographic to match image requirements for the specific platform (see Common Social Media Image Sizes). A properly sized image ensures your audience can view the full image as intended. If you're only using social media to promote your infographic and your audience will click through to view it on a website, you do not need to worry about sizing it to fit size requirements of social media websites. A final consideration for digital infographics is if your audience might download and print an online infographic, then you will want to make sure it is print-friendly.

BOX 5.2. PIXEL DEFINITION AND EXAMPLE

PIXEL DEFINITION

Short for "Picture Element," pixel is the smallest unit of programmable color in a digital image that can be represented on a digital display device. Zooming into an image you will see pixel units represented by small squares or rectangles of color.

The total number of pixels form the display resolution of a digital image. More pixels within a digital image provide more accurate representations of the originally designed image and a higher resolution. With lower resolution, the size of a pixel is larger, less concentrated, making them more visible and resulting in a blocky image referred to as "pixelated (Figure 5.1)." The resolution of a digital image should be appropriate for the device where an image will be displayed, such as a computer, tablet, or mobile phone. (O'Neill, 2016; Sharief, 2020; Techopedia, 2020).

FIGURE 5.1 ■ **Example of Pixelated and High-Resolution Images**

Vertical Versus Horizontal Orientation

When selecting a layout, consider if a vertical or horizonal orientation is most appropriate for the story you want to convey and how the audience will navigate the content. Whether digital or print, vertical orientation is often preferred because people tend to read and scroll from top to bottom of a page (Fessenden, 2018). If the infographic will live online in a digital format, a vertical layout should not exceed 750 pixels in width (may vary by online platform) and 5,000 pixels in height (3,300 pixels equals 11 inches, or about one printed page length; Krum, 2014; McCready, 2017; see Pixel Definition). Any longer than this, and your audience may begin to experience a reduction in comprehension and lose sight of the central message of your info-graphic (Sanchez & Wiley, 2009).

Horizontal layouts can be visually appealing and appropriate for infographics where the main focal point is oriented horizontally, such as an annotated or interactive map of the United States or a historical visual timeline. If printed, a horizontally oriented infographic should fit on letter-sized paper in a landscape layout. If your audience will view a horizontally oriented infographic online, the width of the online platform, typically 750 pixels, will dictate the width of the infographic. Horizontal infographics can be less conducive to reading online, particularly on mobile devices, when they require audiences to scroll left and right to review the full content (Krum, 2014). Fitting a horizontal infographic within an online platform could require reducing the overall size of the infographic, which could make viewing the infographic more difficult for audiences. However, you can make a digital, horizontally oriented infographic easily readable for your audience by including pop-up boxes or a zoom feature that readers can use to navigate and easily review the infographic's content.

Infographic Posters

Infographic posters, such as those presented at professional conferences, are an effective way to visually communicate information to audiences in a printed format, vertically or horizontally. They provide ample space for infographic content, yet still necessitate a well-organized layout. Inserting too much information into a large-sized infographic without a structured layout can confuse, distract, or detract from the central message. You can use large page sizes to create an infographic poster, such as four feet (height) by five feet (wide), a common size for conference posters. As with all infographics, you will want to adjust your page size and layout settings in the design software you use before you begin to build the infographic. Most online template websites will allow you to resize your infographic to poster size. This should be done before beginning to modify the online template to ensure elements are properly sized. Different online template websites offer varying resizing capabilities. For example, Canva offers resizing for paid accounts, while Venngage and Piktochart offer resizing for free accounts.

When printing in a poster-sized format, consider how visuals and text will display. If you enlarge a small infographic that was originally created for a report, the visuals and text will appear much larger than what would be appropriate in a poster-sized infographic. For example, a close-up photograph of a person's face might be fine when printed in letter size, but imagine how large the same image would be if displayed in a poster. Keep in mind low-resolution visu-als could appear pixelated if enlarged from a smaller size, and the use of white space could seem overexaggerated when scaled to poster size. Conversely, if your infographic includes a large amount of information and intricate data visualization, such as *The Basics of Early Childhood Development* poster by Eleanor Lutz for Nerdcore Medical, a large-sized infographic allows readers to easily view detailed information up close (Figure 5.2).

FIGURE 5.2 ■ Eleanor Lutz's Poster of *The Basics of Early Childhood Development* for Nerdcore Medical

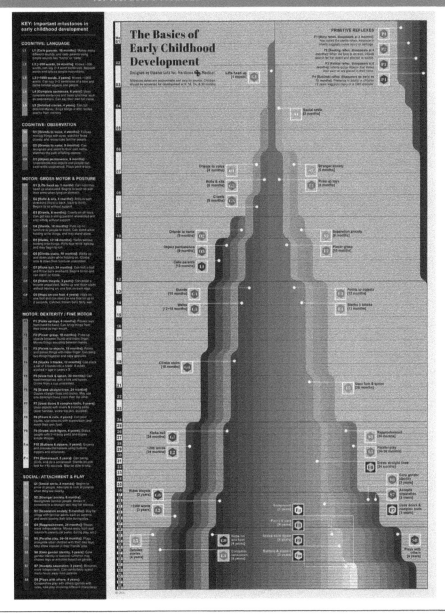

Eleanor Lutz for Nerdcore Medical

LAYOUTS FOR DIFFERENT LEVELS OF AUDIENCE INTERACTION

You can design infographic layouts with attention to how your audience will interact with the visual content that communicates your infographic's story and purpose. Static infographics tend to be the most common design with simple formatting when saved as an image (e.g., .jpg, .png, .svg) for use in a Word or PDF file or online. Static infographics are also easy to share and disseminate through email and social media without the need of additional software applications or browser plugins (Krum, 2014). However, you might amplify your infographic story by increasing audience interface through clickable, animated, video, or interactive features.

Clickable Infographics

While most infographics are static because of their ease of design and portability, you might consider other layout features and formats that communicate your infographic's story and visualize data in different ways. One such way is to incorporate clickable or hoverable elements. For example, one design feature involves embedding hyperlinks in a static infographic that take the audience to an online PDF document or other URL address where they can find more information. This type of clickable infographic keeps the infographic's design clean and concise and removes details that might detract the reader from the central message. Clickable or hoverable popup elements embedded in an infographic also provide an opportunity to provide additional information within a design. For example, the *Lunar Cycle and Sleep* infographic by Rebecca Bergh uses visuals with hover functionality that allows the audience to interact with the content to see how sleep characteristics vary based on the moon's cycle (Figure 5.3). The hover feature in this infographic demonstrates an appropriate use of an interactive element that increases audience engagement and maximizes the use of space to present content. Infographics with a zoom feature allow the audience to navigate a large, complex infographic by zooming in to read its details. A zooming interface is appropriate for large static designs where the full content is not readable online and where you want the audience to see the big picture of the story before delving into its details (Krum, 2014).

Animated Infographics

Infographics animated with a GIF image file format offer another interface for attracting the audience's attention through movement of design visuals, such as showing a sequence or step in a process or depicting changes in spatial relations over time. As alluring as they may be, animated infographics may not enhance comprehension or memory recall of information more than static infographics because the mind might not process information at the same speed of the animation and because animations risk misrepresenting information, thus resulting in misinterpretation (Tversky, 2005). When considering animations for an infographic's layout, make sure they help the audience perceive and understand the central message your story is trying to convey. Eleanor Lutz creates beautiful infographics that incorporate animations for illustrative purposes, such as mapping a wingbeat across five flying species to show different patterns (Figure 5.4).

FIGURE 5.3 ■ *Lunar Sleep Cycle* Infographic With Hover Example

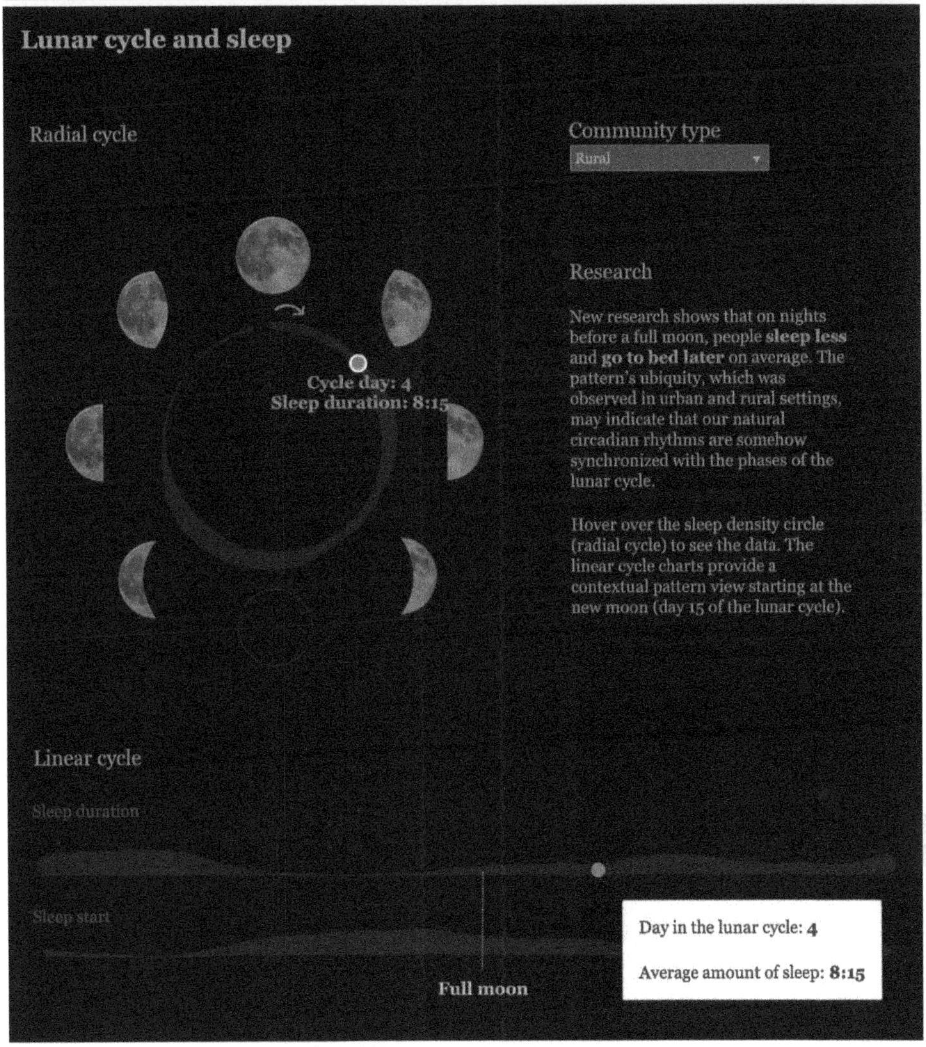

Rebecca Bergh, University of Washington, 2021

Video Infographics

Video infographics provide another engaging visual interface for audiences. The presentation software application you use, such as Microsoft PowerPoint, Prezi, or Canva, will influence what kinds of layouts are available. For example, an online video infographic template from Canva might have a preset layout, whereas in PowerPoint, you can customize the slide size and layout, and use animations and timed slide transitions to create a video. A video infographic designed in presentation software can be saved as a video file and shared through sites like

FIGURE 5.4 ■ **Still Image of Eleanor Lutz's Animated Infographic** *Flight Videos Deconstructed*

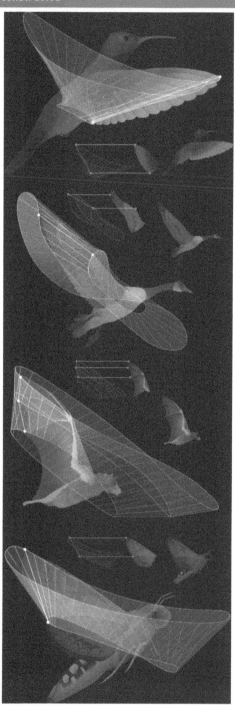

FIGURE 5.5   ■   Still Image of UNICEF's *Children of the Recession* Video

YouTube and Vimeo (Krum, 2014). Despite this different visual interface, all design elements discussed in Steps 1 through 7 apply to video infographics. UNICEF effectively uses a video infographic, *Children of the Recession*, to show its story of how the great recession has resulted in greater poverty levels among children in developed countries (Figure 5.5). The video leverages visual effects to present complex information and data in a compelling, digestible, and memorable way (https://www.youtube.com/watch?v=A_zTNh7wino).

Interactive Infographics

Interactive infographics provide an interface that actively engages the audience with selecting how to view data visualizations and information in different ways. These infographics require the use of software programs, such as Tableau and Power Bi, which pull your data to create interactive visualizations that can be embedded in a website or a larger infographic design (Krum, 2014). If you believe your infographic story is best told through an interactive interface, then at this step in the development process, it is important to consider the design layouts available through the software program you will use. Keep in mind the layout should support the central message of your infographic's story and how you want the audience to navigate the story. Interactive infographics, while seemingly engaging, could risk telling the story in a way that exceeds readers' cognitive resources by requiring them to coordinate and split their attention between the different elements of the infographic (Greussing & Boomgaarden, 2021). Ideally, the story should drive choices in layout and not the other way around.

With interactive infographics, however, the audience most often creates the story, and the developer sets the stage for the story through access to tools to interact with data. The interactive function allows users to explore data visualizations based on their interests, questions, or intent for accessing the infographic. The *270 to Win's 2024 Presidential Election Interactive Map* allows users to create their own story using the map's interactivity to forecast electoral vote outcomes (Figure 5.6). After creating their map, users can share their forecasted story through various dissemination outlets, including social media (https://www.270towin.com/).

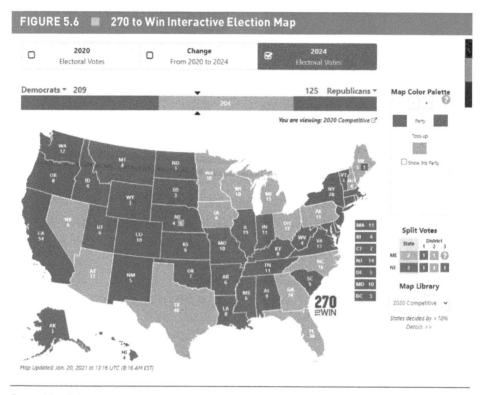

FIGURE 5.6   270 to Win Interactive Election Map

Source: Allan Keiter

The following are considerations for determining appropriate level of audience interaction through an infographic's layout:

- Review the amount of content and visuals you identified in Steps 3 and 4 and gauge if the volume of information will fit within the page size for your infographic. This will become clearer when you start to build the infographic in Step 8, but being mindful of it in the planning phase will help you determine your options for organizing information.

- Use hyperlinks, clickable popups, or hover features that offer the audience access to more detailed information in an unobtrusive way that minimizes visual clutter.

- Overengineering an infographic with animated or interactive embellishments risks distracting the audience's attention from the central message. Select animated and interactive features only when they are integral to communicating your infographic's story.

- Determine if you have the requisite skills, budget, and time for integrating animated or interactive features into your infographic. Envisioning is one thing. Executing is another.

LAYOUTS FOR DIFFERENT STORIES

Once you consider the appropriate size, orientation, and level of interaction for your infographic, you will select a layout that organizes the information on the page in the simplest and most navigable way to tell your story. Certain layouts work better for different types of stories. It is wise to choose a layout that will be conducive to your story because it will help the viewer process the information and central message in a logical way. Examples of common layout types include hierarchical/sequential, categorical, comparison, timeline, and descriptive (Figure 5.7).

FIGURE 5.7 ■ Examples of Infographic Layouts		
Type	**Layout Structure**	**Description**
Hierarchical/ Sequential	Step 1 / Step 2 / Step 3	This layout is best for an infographic showing a relationship among key pieces of information, such as steps in an evaluation. The visuals cues to indicate a hierarchical layout could involve sequential sections, or ascending numbers.
Categorical		This layout is best for presenting different categories of information. For example, you may be creating an infographic on the six recommendations for program developers based on your evaluation. Certain visual cues can be used to separate the different categories, such as placing each recommendation in its own section, or using color to differentiate the categories.
Comparative		This type of infographic would work well when comparing two groups, such as treatment and control groups in a study, side by side. In this layout, the viewer recognizes the comparison of two groups by having each group in a column, and then each specific attribute is compared row by row.
Timeline		A timeline infographic presents a visual sequence of events over time. Each point in the timeline is represented visually. It can capture evaluation activities, data points, or program history or implementation over time, for example.
Descriptive		More often than not, you are telling a story descriptively with a beginning, middle, and end. The main points of your story might not have a relationship to each other that would benefit from a layout designed to show those relationships. With this type of infographic, you can be creative with how you organize information within the layout while using visual cues to help your reader navigate the content.

Infographic templates from the online website, Canva, offer examples of each layout in Figure 5.8. Each example shows how visual cues, such as colors, dividers, and captions, help readers prioritize and locate important information for the infographic's story (Malamed, 2009).

FIGURE 5.8   ■   Five Examples of Infographic Layouts

Five Infographic Layouts

Hierarchical/ Sequential

Categorical

Comparative

Descriptive

Timeline

CREATING BALANCE IN THE LAYOUT

An infographic's layout provides a foundation for organizing information in a way that helps the reader easily navigate through the infographic and comprehend its message. When an infographic has balance, the layout emphasizes the main points so readers know where to focus their attention (see Maintaining Balance Beyond Step 5).

BOX 5.3. MAINTAINING BALANCE
BEYOND STEP 5

Seeking balance in your infographic doesn't stop at Step 5. It's important to remember that you will continue to revisit your design choices throughout Steps 5 to 10 to see if you've maintained balance.

The following are considerations for creating balance in a layout:

- Condense and organize information into digestible "chunks," or sections.

- Size sections to represent the relative importance of information for the infographic's message. The larger the section, the more important the point.

- Place sections on a page in a way that emphasizes the focal point.

- Use white space to help infographic sections flow together.

Each of these considerations is discussed in the following sections.

Layout Sections

Dividing your infographic into sections will help organize the presentation of information in a purposeful way. There is no rule as to the number of sections to include in an infographic, but this is where balance comes into play. In design, the rule of thirds often applies to art, graphic design, and print media among other forms of design. An infographic can also apply this design principle by dividing the page into thirds using a grid (Beegel, 2014). This also corresponds to how one might typically organize a story with an introduction, main point, and conclusion (Figure 5.9). Your sections can be organized symmetrically or asymmetrically, as long as the balance of your infographic is maintained. The rule of thirds can apply to both symmetrical and asymmetrical oriented layouts, while maintaining balance in either orientation.

Determining the number of sections for the infographic's layout will depend on the number and types of visual elements you identified to show your story in Step 4. Too many sections, however, will clutter your infographic and make it difficult to discern the central message (Figure 5.10).

FIGURE 5.9   ■   Section Layout Examples Using Rule of Thirds

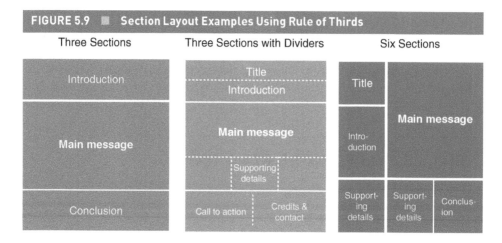

FIGURE 5.10   ■   Too Many Sections

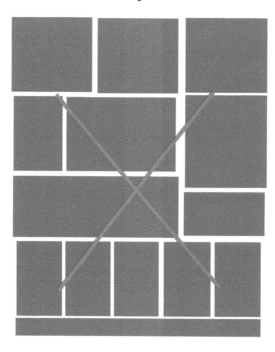

Layout Section Size

Your decision for how to size each section should be directly related to the relative importance of the information in that section. A balanced layout gives each story element the appropriate amount of visual space relative to its importance in the story. This visual hierarchy gives the viewers cues to what information they should be paying attention (Malamed, 2009). A larger section should be given for the main point, whereas the introduction, supporting details, and conclusion can be housed in smaller sections. If you are presenting pieces of information of equal importance, consider using equally sized sections.

Section Placement

The location of each section in your infographic will vary based on the flow of your story. There is also a logical placement for the main sections of an infographic's story. For a vertical-oriented layout, the title and introduction will likely be placed toward the top of the infographic. The middle sections will most likely include your central message and your focal point. Sections with supporting details may follow after, or be near, your central message sections. The conclusion, call to action, and references will likely be at the bottom of the infographic.

White Space

White space is your friend, and should be used intentionally in an infographic. White space is any area free from text or images and can be any color. The use of white space is subjective and artistic in its effect and can be active or passive. Active white space is often asymmetrical, which helps a design look dynamic and moves the eye across the infographic, while passive white space is the normal white space that occurs in between words on a line or around an image (Boulton, 2007). It can be tempting to stuff your infographic full of information, especially if it is based on a study with several findings and other information that seems important to share. However, using active and passive white space has many benefits and can increase comprehension of the information presented in the infographic. When used properly, white space can highlight important elements in the infographic and lead the reader's eye from one thing to another. White space also gives the reader a bit of breathing room; it can be distracting and confusing to have an infographic full of disconnected information. Instead of trying to say too much, one rule to remember is "less can be more." For example, the USDA comparison infographic delineating differences between the Dietary Guidelines Advisory Committee Report and the Dietary Guidelines for Americans uses white space between and within each section of the infographic, thus limiting visual distractions and directing the eye to the most important information in each section of the infographic (Figure 5.11).

FIGURE 5.11 ■ **Example Comparison Infographic With Use of White Space to Create Balance**

United States Department of Agriculture

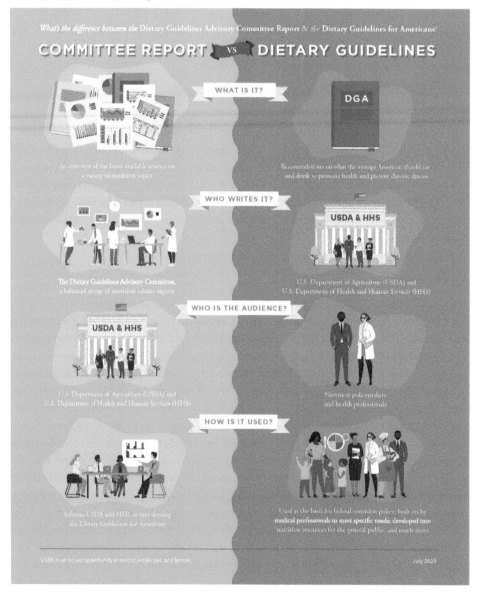

Source: United States Department of Agriculture, 2020

BOX 5.4. STEP 5 DESIGN CHALLENGE

DESIGN CHALLENGE: WHAT IF I'M UNSURE WHICH LAYOUT IS MOST APPROPRIATE FOR THE CENTRAL MESSAGE?

When you consider the story and visual elements you identified in Steps 3 and 4, it might not be obvious which layout features would best communicate the infographic's central message. Multiple layouts could work for communicating your infographic's story, *so how do you narrow it down to one*?

Ask yourself how your main points and supporting details relate to each other. Is there a linear relationship where the central message builds through multiple consecutive points? Consider a hierarchical layout. Does the story have a time element that is integral to conveying the central message? Consider a timeline layout. Are you comparing two groups or programs to each other? Use a comparison layout. If you have multiple main points that are equally important, a categorical layout might work best. If none of these layouts apply, a descriptive layout will give you flexibility in organizing your content. With a descriptive layout, use the rule of thirds to size and place infographic sections.

A hybrid layout might be most appropriate. There is no need to force content into a predetermined layout if it isn't purposeful and helpful in the development process. When elements of different layouts make sense given the nature of the infographic's story, integrating both is an option. Make sure, however, the layout still adheres to guidelines for balance.

Keep sight of how your audience will access and interface with the infographic. If you want to embed interactive features into the layout, make sure your audience can utilize them. If your audience will only see the infographic in print form, then integrating interactivity would be inappropriate. Consider if your audience will have equitable access to adequate Internet connectivity that enables them to view infographic videos or GIF images and use interactive dashboards.

Remember this is an iterative process. Selecting a layout in Step 5 establishes a framework for organizing information. It is your starting point that will evolve as you construct the infographic in Step 8. As your layout evolves, you will want to revisit guidelines for creating balance in your infographic in Step 5.

BOX 5.5. PLANETS ILLUSTRATIVE EXAMPLE— SELECT LAYOUT

At this point in the development process, we have identified our infographic's audience, purpose, story, data, and visuals. Now in Step 5 we consider how the infographic's layout can serve to present the PLANETS story in an organized and navigable manner. Let's first revisit the central message for the PLANETS infographic that we articulated in Step 3:

PLANETS activities build learners' habits of mind and improve their attitudes toward engineering by engaging them in collaborative problem-solving through an engineering design process.

Two main points support the story's central message, so we had a few considerations for selecting an appropriate layout. First, we looked at the relationship between the two main points and determined that one point—demonstrating habits of mind—would lead to the second point—increasing positive attitudes toward engineering. A timeline was not part of the story nor were we making any comparisons or describing information categorically. We chose a hybrid layout that was predominately descriptive, but also integrated a hierarchical element given the relationship between the two main points.

Because the infographic presented findings from a comprehensive evaluation report, we made a couple other layout determinations. As a companion document, we wanted the infographic to be the same size as the report. We also considered that the intended audience might print the infographic along with the evaluation report, so we restricted its dimensions to letter size (8.5 inches by 11 inches). In revisiting our narrative and visual content from Steps 3 and 4, we also realized we had more information than what a letter-sized infographic would likely accommodate. Considering our time and resources for developing the infographic, we decided that hyperlinks would be the easiest and most cost-effective way to provide the audience with access to more information supporting its content. We wanted to keep it simple because of the amount of information in the data visualizations, so we decided not to include any other interactive features.

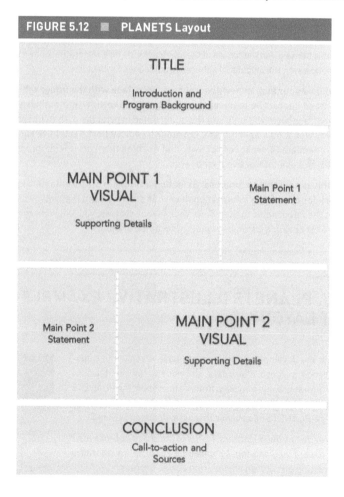

FIGURE 5.12 ■ PLANETS Layout

With the hybrid layout, we plotted simple lines to divide the infographic into sections using the rule of thirds (Figure 5.12). While still early in the design process, we demarcated sections for the main story elements with consideration of the PLANETS visual components we identified in Step 4. Based on our assessment of visual relevance, we created the largest sections in equal size for the two main points in hierarchical order from top to bottom. We segmented smaller sections for the introduction and conclusion sections, which combined, represent one third of the infographic.

Using this layout as a guide, we have a starting point for organizing information on the page. We know once we begin building the infographic in Step 8, we might change aspects of the layout to achieve balance and navigability. Beginning with a roadmap, however, will help us winnow complex amounts of information into digestible chunks that communicate a compelling story.

NOW IT'S YOUR TURN!

- Find an infographic online (for example, see Eleanor Lutz's static and animated infographics at https://tabletopwhale.com/archive.html or visit infographic design templates from Adobe Express at https://www.adobe.com/express/discover/examples/infographic) and explore if you can identify the following:
  - the type of infographic layout (hierarchical/sequential, categorical, comparison, timeline, descriptive)
  - adherence with the rule of thirds
  - use of white space
  - balance among sections of the layout

- Find examples of infographics with interactive features, such as zooming, clickable, video, and interactive dashboards. Evaluate whether you believe the interactive feature enhances communication of the central message or distracts from it. Is there anything you would change to improve the value of the interactive feature in conveying the central message? How would removing the interactive feature affect the infographic's attractiveness and understandability?

- Select your layout for your infographic. Revisit the story elements and visual components you identified in Steps 3 and 4, and considering the guidelines presented in Step 5, identify the type of layout that might be appropriate for your infographic's content as well as how you might segment story elements on the page.

RESOURCES

Check it out!

- ZoomIt annotation and zooming tool for infographics: https://zoomit.en.softonic.com/

- Guide to making GIFs for infographics by Tabletop Whale: https://tabletopwhale.com/2014/11/03/how-to-make-an-animated-infographic.html

- 10 Rules of Composition All Designers Live by: https://www.canva.com/learn/visual-design-composition/

- How to Use the Rule of Thirds Effortlessly: https://www.companyfolders.com/blog/rule-of-thirds-graphic-design

NOTES

1. It is not recommended that you create your infographic in a word processing program, such as Microsoft Word or Pages. We recommend developing your infographic in a program more suitable to graphic design, such as Microsoft PowerPoint, Adobe Illustrator, or an online template (e.g., Canva, Venngage, and Piktochart) and saving it as an image that can be embedded in a text document. See Step 8 for more information on infographic design platforms.

STEP 6: CHOOSE DESIGN ELEMENTS

LEARNING OBJECTIVES

In Step 6, you will learn how to

- identify a color scheme that helps communicate infographic content with the audience in mind,

- apply colors consistently to elements in an infographic,

- select typefaces and font treatments that are congruent and harmonious with infographic content,

- create flow in your infographic using visual cues that create a navigational pathway through the infographic, and

- be intentional about using a focal point that grabs the audience's attention and draws the reader into an infographic.

After considering the structural layout of your infographic in Step 5, the next step involves identifying your visual story's design elements. In Step 6, you will select a color scheme and fonts and apply them to the visual elements you identified in Step 4. An infographic's layout designates how you will divide information on a page to organize the space for presenting your infographic's story. With a structural layout in place, you can choose your infographic's design elements to bring stylistic coherence and flow to your infographic's central message.

While major design decisions are important, such as what visuals to include, additional design choices, such as color, font, flow, and focal point, can make a difference in effectively communicating an infographic's story. Effective design elements captivate the audience's attention and direct it to the infographic's central message. An infographic's design elements should promote readability and organize information with visual cues that help readers navigate through the story. When design elements work together to create a sense of visual harmony in an infographic, the reader can focus on the content of the story, free of visual distraction. A well-designed and aesthetically appealing visual display of information is associated with holding an audience's attention and building trust in its content (Cyr, 2008; Djamasbi et al., 2010).

As you contemplate design elements for your infographic in Step 6, ask yourself, "Does this choice support the central message and purpose of the infographic? Will it resonate with my audience?" Determining these elements in advance will result in an infographic with greater coherence, clarity, and relevance for your audience.

USING COLOR INTENTIONALLY

Color is a powerful design element in an infographic for capturing your audience's attention immediately. Increased attention creates arousal in our brain, which helps us remember what we saw (Anderson & Bowman, 2018; Dzulkifli & Mustafar, 2013; Spence et al., 2006). For example, red is a color we pay attention to as it can convey importance or urgency (e.g., stop signs or danger signals), influence our preferences, and affect our appetites (Kuhbandner et al., 2015). Many fast-food chains use red in their branding, namely to make a memorable impression that influences potential customers to purchase a product (Anderson & Bowman, 2018). Between 62% to 90% of consumers subconsciously judge an environment or product based on color alone within 90 seconds of initial viewing (WebFX, 2022). Thus, using color strategically in an infographic can grab the audience's attention and help them recall information later. However, using color to attract the audience's attention is only one consideration for selecting colors for an infographic.

Color can influence human emotions in a positive or negative manner depending on what the audience associates with a color (Hemphill, 1996; Elliott, 2015; Palmer & Schloss, 2011). Warm colors (e.g., red, orange, and yellow) may stimulate intense or heated feelings, whereas cool colors (e.g., purple, blue, and green) may evoke more restful and peaceful emotions (Ballast, 2002; Jonauskaite et al., 2019). Consider what affective response you want to elicit through your infographic. If you want to excite an audience about the infographic's message, consider a brighter, colorful palette with pink, turquoise, and yellow, for example (Bartram et al., 2017). To convey a sense of calmness or security, choose a softer, muted palette with blues and greens (Naz & Helen, 2004). If you want to evoke dissenting feelings about a social justice topic, for example, you might use a contrasting palette with black, red, and white.

Your audience's social and cultural backgrounds can also influence their emotional association with colors and the symbolic relevance and meaning they ascribe to specific colors (Jonauskaite et al., 2019; Mukherjee et al., 2022). When used intentionally and appropriately, colors can elicit feelings of pride, loyalty, and belonging because they symbolically represent a positive and significant association for the audience. Conversely, colors might communicate the wrong symbolic message and evoke a negative emotional response. Using color intentionally involves understanding the meaning and significance of colors for the audience based on their culture and community. If you are reaching an audience associated with a specific country, religion, institution, or a movement, for example, you will want to be sensitive to the preferences and meaning your audience ascribes to colors based on their social and cultural context (Palmer & Schloss, 2011). For example, the color red has been associated with danger or anger in the United States; good luck, fortune, and fertility in Asian communities; mourning in some African communities; and protection and happiness among Native American communities (Jonauskaite et al., 2019; Singh, 2006). Yellow represents benevolence in Ukraine; mourning in Mexico, Egypt, and Ethiopia; and courage in Japan (Aslam, 2006). Social movements are also represented by colors; for example, pink typically represents breast cancer awareness, a rainbow of colors represents various versions of Pride and LGBTQIA+ flags, and black has been the singular color of the Black Lives Matter movement in the United States.

In sum, one color can be associated with many different emotions and concepts, and many colors can be associated with one emotion or concept (Schloss et al., 2018). There can be both universality and cultural specificity of color associations, and they are highly context-dependent (Schloss et al., 2018). The association between colors and their possible meanings or cultural representations can also vary in magnitude (strongly or weakly associated) and emotional investment (positive or negative). Therefore, researching the background of your audience (see Step 1) can help inform your selection of colors.

Selecting a Color Scheme

Several considerations contribute to the color scheme for an infographic. These include the number of colors for an infographic, color associations with an infographic's topic, branding, and color accessibility, such as colorblindness and printing in black and white. As a general guide, a color scheme should consist of a simple palette with no more than three to four colors or different saturations of one or two colors across text and visualizations. Using fewer rather than more colors keeps visual distractions to a minimum. Selecting a color scheme that is difficult to view may reduce the overall readability of your infographic (Richardson et al., 2014).

Colors Connected to Topics. When selecting a color scheme for your infographic, consider the audience's potential associations between colors and the infographic's topic. By understanding the audience's background and any color associations with a topic, you can use color as a strategic and intentional design element. This will also inform how many colors you use and how you apply them to visuals and text in your infographic.

If the topic of your infographic pertains to a specific social, cultural, political, or religious group, research the colors commonly associated with that topic and consider how to incorporate the colors in the infographic. For example, George Mason University's infographic titled *U.S. Foreign-Born Population and the 2018 Midterm Elections* uses typical colors people associate with the Democrat and Republican political parties—blue and red, respectively. The consistent color treatment applies to the data visualizations and the corresponding text (Figure 6.1). The use of color in the infographic helps readers quickly and easily distinguish differences between the two groups. This helps the audience ascertain the infographic's central message about the majority of the foreign-born population living in states with a Democratic governor.

If the topic of an infographic is specific to a country, then investigate the colors associated with the social, cultural, and religious background of its citizens. For example, Just Hope International created the infographic, *The Country and People of Ghana*, to educate audiences about the country (Figure 6.2). It incorporates the colors of the national flag (red, gold, and green) and uses gradations of the predominate color gold, which represents the mineral wealth of the country (National Symbols, n.d.).

FIGURE 6.1 ▦ *U.S. Foreign-Born Population and the 2018 Midterm Elections Infographic*

U.S. Foreign-Born Population and the 2018 Midterm Elections

After the 2018 midterm elections, **27 states have Republican governors** and **23 states have Democratic governors.**
In states with Republican governors, 10.5% of the total population is foreign born.
In states with Democratic governors, 15.6% of the total population is foreign born.

26.6 million foreign-born individuals live in states **with Democratic governors.**
15.5 million live in states **with Republican governors.**

Naturalized Citizens, by Party of Governor

13.2 million naturalized citizens live in states with Democratic governors.
6.8 million naturalized citizens live in states with Republican governors.

63% of the total foreign-born population lives in states with Democratic governors, while **37%** lives in states with Republican governors.

Source: George Mason University Institute for Immigration Research

FIGURE 6.2 ■ *The Country and People of Ghana* Infographic

If a specific object or concept represents the topic of an infographic, consider using universally associated colors with that object or concept. For example, people commonly associate water with the color blue, so if the topic is about water, using blue in the color scheme helps readers recall that the infographic was about water. If you search online for infographics about water, you'll find the majority of them include shades of blue, similar to the infographic titled, *Water Scarcity by the Numbers* by Waterlogic (Figure 6.3). This infographic applies four shades of blue

---

FIGURE 6.3 ■ *Water Scarcity by the Numbers* **Infographic**

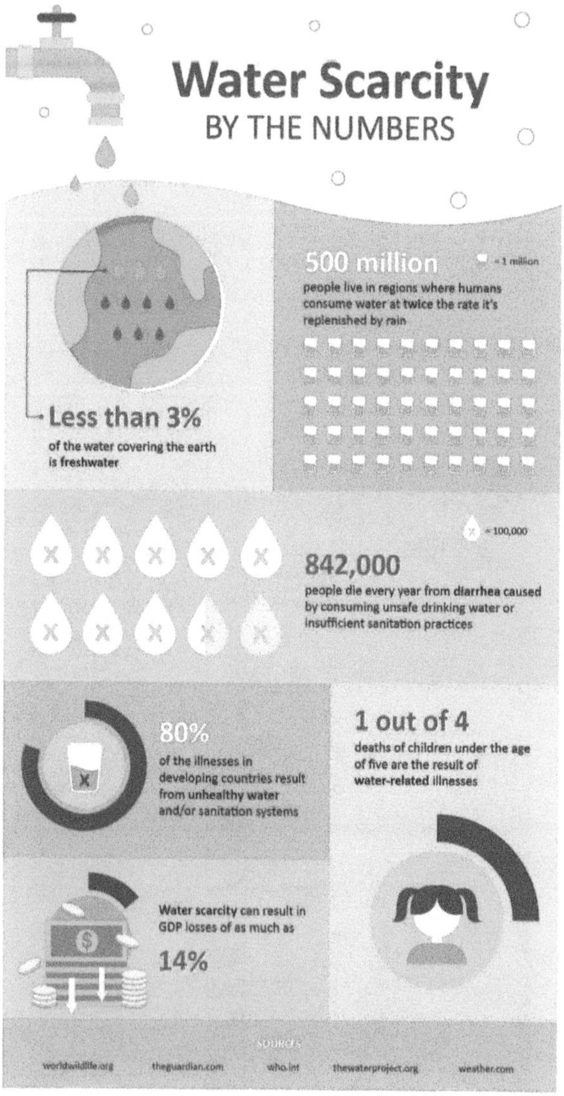

Water Scarcity
BY THE NUMBERS

Less than 3%
of the water covering the earth
is freshwater

500 million
people live in regions where humans
consume water at twice the rate it's
replenished by rain

● = 1 million

● = 100,000

842,000
people die every year from diarrhea caused
by consuming unsafe drinking water or
insufficient sanitation practices

80%
of the illnesses in
developing countries result
from unhealthy water
and/or sanitation systems

1 out of 4
deaths of children under the age
of five are the result of
water-related illnesses

Water scarcity can result in
GDP losses of as much as
14%

SOURCES

worldwildlife.org   theguardian.com   who.int   thewaterproject.org   weather.com

---

Source: Waterlogic

to text, data visualizations, and section background shading with the added "pop" color of violet to highlight key data points. The multiple treatment applications of the color blue create coherence and visual appeal while reinforcing the audiences' association of blue with the infographic's story about water scarcity.

If the infographic's topic represents a brand, such as for a product, program, or organization, using the brand colors in your infographic can create coherence not only within the infographic, but across other communication assets and materials for that brand. When selecting a color scheme from brand colors, be sensitive to associations your audience might have with those colors and the strength of those associations. Also consider how well the color combinations within a brand complement or contrast with one another. Some brand colors offer limited options for an infographic either because there are only one or two main colors or the colors would not be visually appealing or harmonious used in saturation throughout an infographic (e.g., lime green and black). When this is the case, consider using shaded gradations of one of the branding colors and use the secondary color as an accent to attract the audience's eye. If you select a brand's color scheme, you will need the exact color codes for the branded colors. See the section on color codes later in this chapter.

Color Palettes. What if there is no topic, concept, emotion, or color association to help you select a color palette? Or what if you have one color in mind but are unsure what colors might complement it for an infographic? Several online websites generate color palettes. Websites, such as Coolors.co and Adobe Color, can generate color palettes from a single color, explore existing palettes, and extract colors from an existing image to create a color palette. They also include accessibility tools to test colors for colorblindness and contrast between text and background colors. These sites are intuitive and easy to use, and are worth incorporating into your design process (see Design Resource "How To": Generate Colors with Coolors.co).

BOX 6.1. DESIGN RESOURCE "HOW TO": GENERATE COLORS WITH COOLORS.CO

DESIGN RESOURCE "HOW TO"

Generate Colors With Coolors.co

Coolors.co allows the user to explore color options by generating palettes from a single color or image. You can also peruse existing palettes for inspiration.

- **Generate color palette.** Use this feature to explore random color palettes or customize a specific color palette. Press your spacebar to shuffle among colors. Coolors.co defaults to five colors, but press the "X" to delete a color from the palette. If you like a color, use the lock button to "freeze" it and keep it in the shuffle. Take note of **the HEX (hexadecimal) code** (Figure 6.4). If you want to use this code, simply copy and paste it in your online infographic template or PowerPoint custom color box.

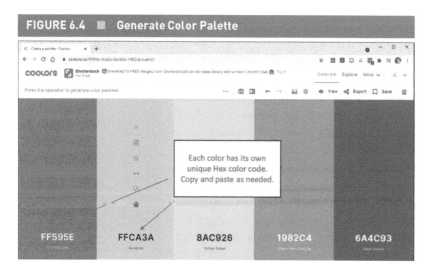

FIGURE 6.4 ■ Generate Color Palette

Each color has its own unique Hex color code. Copy and paste as needed.

FF595E   FFCA3A   8AC926   1982C4   6A4C93

- **Generate method:** Here you can select what type of color palette interests you (Figure 6.5). The default will be "Auto," which means random color selection. Other options include a monochromatic color palette, which means different shades of one color. If you want a more vibrant color palette composed of complementary colors, see colors opposite from each other on the color wheel. Any of these color scheme methods will work for generating a simple pallet of three to four colors your infographic. Remember to examine them for appropriate color accessibility and contrast.

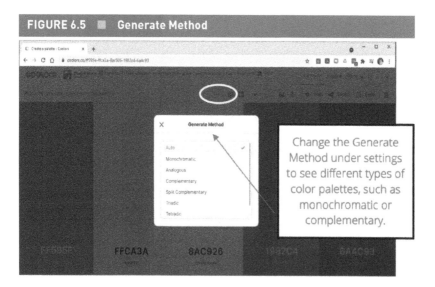

FIGURE 6.5 ■ Generate Method

Change the Generate Method under settings to see different types of color palettes, such as monochromatic or complementary.

- **Explore existing color palettes.** If you're feeling stumped, explore existing color palettes other Coolors.co users created (Figure 6.6). This might be a helpful place to go for inspiration.

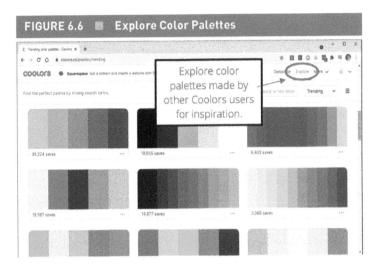

FIGURE 6.6 ■ **Explore Color Palettes**

Explore color palettes made by other Coolors users for inspiration.

- **Upload image to get color:** Uploading an image is helpful to identify colors and their color codes within a featured image or an organization's logo if using branding colors (Figure 6.7). If you don't have an image file of an organization's logo or brand colors, you can take a screen shot of an organization's website or logo and upload the image to identify the colors. Here, we upload an image to Coolors.co and drag the cursor over the image to identify specific colors and view them in our color palette.

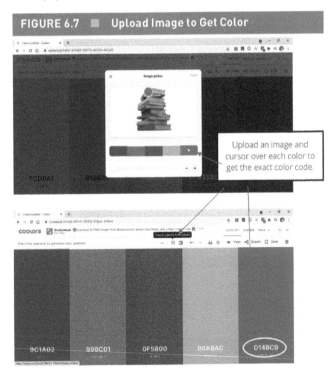

FIGURE 6.7 ■ **Upload Image to Get Color**

Upload an image and cursor over each color to get the exact color code.

Color Codes. Every color has a unique color code that differentiates it from other colors. Color codes allow us to use exact colors, which creates consistency and coherence in your infographic. For example, the *U.S. Foreign-Born Population and the 2018 Midterm Elections* infographic uses different shades of blue for the title background, map, and charts but could improve visual consistency by using the same color code when creating different infographic elements in blue (Figure 6.8). Color codes are helpful when branding an infographic or extracting a color from an existing image, such as a logo. The two main color codes you will use during infographic development are RGB and HEX color codes.

- **RGB** color codes consist of three numbers representing red, green, and blue. For example, (170, 74, 68) is the RGB code for the color Brick Red. If you are working in an online application or Microsoft Office to create your infographic, you will be able to use an RGB code.

- A **HEX** code is another common color code used in creating infographics. HEX stands for hexadecimal, and this type of code is a six-digit combination of numbers and letters that represent a color. Hex codes start with the pound sign (#). For example, Brick Red has a HEX code of #AA4A44. Most infographic template websites and online resources will require you to use a HEX code.

FIGURE 6.8 ■ *U.S. Foreign-Born Population and the 2018 Midterm Elections Infographic*

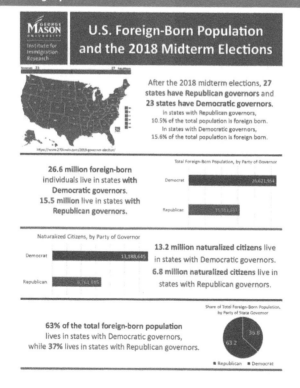

Each color will have both an RGB and HEX code. If needed, websites can translate one type of color code into another, such as RGB to HEX Color Converter (https://www.rgbtohex. net/). Other less common color codes that you may encounter include CMYK (Cyan, Magenta, Yellow, and Black) for printing and HSL (Hue, Saturation, Lightness; Kirk, 2016).

Color Accessibility. To ensure the audience can view your infographic as intended, be mindful of color accessibility. This includes considerations for color contrast between background colors and text, black-and-white printing, and colorblindness. When considering background colors in an infographic, the contrast between the text color and background color should be distinct.

For example, a dark text color against a dark background would be difficult to read. Instead, choose a lighter color against a dark background, or a dark text color against a light background. In the *Water Scarcity by the Numbers* infographic, the color contrast could be improved between the blue background shading and the violet "pop" color by making the violet a brighter shade of pink or perhaps replacing it with the bright yellow used for the coins (Figure 6.9). The large size of the violet-colored font, however, helps with readability and demonstrates how adjusting font size can also make text more accessible for readers. In addition to Coolors.co and Adobe Color, other websites such as WebAIM can help you determine if colors for background and text have sufficient contrast (see Design Resource "How To": Testing Color Contrasts With WebAIM).

FIGURE 6.9   ■   Smaller version of *Water Scarcity by the Numbers* Infographic

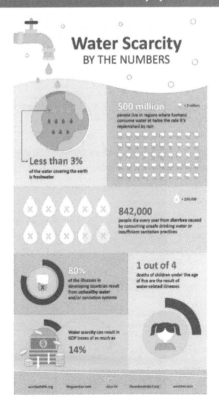

BOX 6.2. DESIGN RESOURCE "HOW TO": TESTING COLOR CONTRASTS WITH WEBAIM

DESIGN RESOURCE "HOW TO"

Testing Color Contrasts With WebAIM

(https://webaim.org/resources/contrastchecker/)

WebAIM allows the user to test color contrasts by entering the HEX code of the text and background colors you intend to use (Figures 6.10 and 6.11). WebAIM will indicate if the color contrasts "pass" the requirements of the Web Content Accessibility Guidelines (WCAG) 2 (Web Accessibility Initiative (WAI), 2022). These standards represent the global goal of improving accessibility for all. Although your infographic may not need to meet these standards, it is still best practice to consider whether audiences can easily view the colors in an infographic.

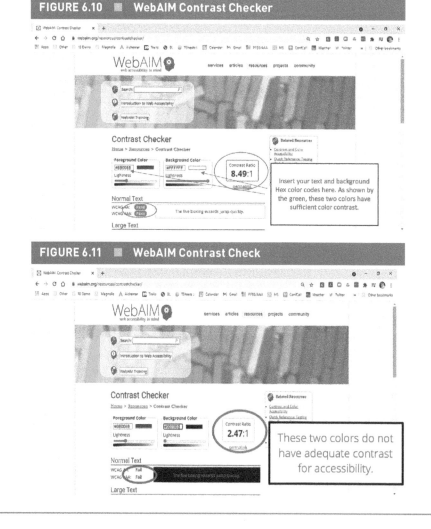

FIGURE 6.10 ■ WebAIM Contrast Checker

Insert your text and background Hex color codes here. As shown by the green, these two colors have sufficient color contrast.

FIGURE 6.11 ■ WebAIM Contrast Check

These two colors do not have adequate contrast for accessibility.

In addition to color contrast, consider how your color choices look printed in black and white. Try mocking up your infographic's color scheme with text and background color, and print it using the greyscale setting on your printer. If the colors do not differentiate well when printed in black and white, increase the contrast between the colors.

Reviewing your color palette for how people with colorblindness will see it is another important consideration for an infographic's accessibility. Colorblindness affects 5% to 8% of males, and less than 1% of females in the United States (Liu, 2010). People who experience colorblindness see colors differently and may not be able to differentiate some colors from one another. The most common type of colorblindness is differentiating between the colors red and green.

Most color websites, including Coolors.co and Adobe Color, include tools to view how your infographic color scheme looks to those who experience colorblindness. Color Brewer 2.0 is another website that allows the user to test colors to see if they are colorblind safe, print friendly, or photocopy safe. Using these color-testing tools helps determine if the audience will easily differentiate the infographic's colors or not (see Design Resource "How To": Color Brewer 2.0).

BOX 6.3. DESIGN RESOURCE "HOW TO": COLOR BREWER 2.0

DESIGN RESOURCE "HOW TO"

Color Brewer 2.0

(https://colorbrewer2.org/)

Use Color Brewer 2.0 to view color palettes that are colorblind safe, print friendly, or photocopy safe (Figure 6.12). The site is designed for mapmakers, but its tools are helpful for

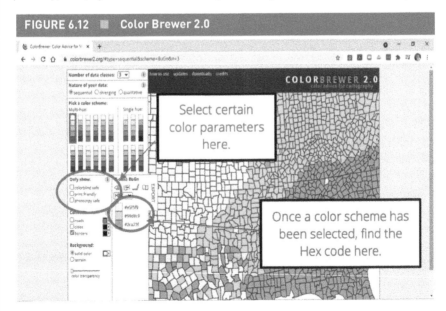

FIGURE 6.12 ■ Color Brewer 2.0

identifying an infographic color palette. Although you can't insert a custom color palette in Color Brewer, you can examine existing ones they display. These palettes represent the differing nature of data, such as data that are sequential (gradations of a single color), diverging (contrasting colors), or qualitative (multiple colors representing different categories).

- Select colorblind safe, print friendly, or photocopy safe for Color Brewer to filter out color palettes based on these criteria. More information about what each of these criteria mean can be found by clicking the "i" in this section.
- **HEX codes** are displayed; simply copy and paste if you want to use the colors shown.

Applying Color to Infographic Elements

Color as a design element creates cohesiveness and visual appeal when applied consistently and intentionally. Color acts as a visual cue to highlight key points in an infographic, link common story elements, and draw the audience's attention to its central message (Babich, 2021). Inconsistent use of color can confuse readers and detract from the visual appeal of your infographic. Additionally, the audience will decode information faster when the applied color matches the actual color of the depicted object (Schloss et al., 2018). For example, a strawberry icon would be red and a plant icon would be green, not the other way around.

When applying color in an infographic, use the same color in consistent ways. For example, if you have multiple key finding statements as headers, use the same color for each. This helps the reader quickly identify that the statements are of equal importance. Supporting text might be in a different color to differentiate it from the rest. Applying one color consistently to the same element throughout an infographic (e.g., section header) creates a visual pattern that makes processing information simpler.

The CDC's infographic, *Invest in Your Community: 4 Considerations to Improve Health and Well-Being for All*, applies a consistent color palette using orange, blue, green, and white as primary colors (Figure 6.13). The infographic balances the color applications in each visual display, thus creating harmony across the four main sections of the infographic. The infographic uses lighter shades of blue to create visual cues that divide sections. Notice also the consistent application of two contrasting colors—white and dark green—for the text and background for the title, section headers, visual labels, and supporting text. The application of color to text and visuals is appealing and consistent, thereby creating visual coherence and drawing attention to the main points. However, if the audience might print the infographic, the blue and green colors are too similar to show contrast in black-and-white printing.

The following are considerations for choosing and applying colors for your infographic:

- Be cognizant that colors coupled with powerful visuals can evoke an emotional or affective response for your audience that will enhance their memory of your infographic. Be intentional with your color choices.

- Select colors through the lens of the audience and what associations they might ascribe to colors based on their social, political, cultural, or religious background.

- Apply color treatments to text, section headers, data visualizations, and other visual elements consistently. Using color codes will help to ensure consistent use of the same color.

- Ensure your color palette is visually accessible to the audience by checking for color contrast, colorblindness, and printing in black and white, if applicable.

FIGURE 6.13 ■ *Invest in Your Community* **Infographic**

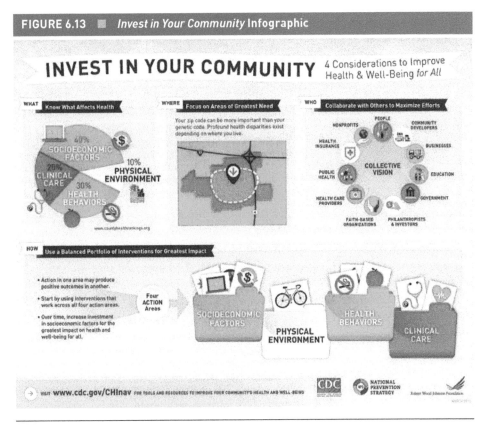

Source: Center for Disease Control

SELECTING HARMONIOUS FONTS

Like color, fonts can add visual cohesiveness and appeal to an infographic, or they can distract or repel the reader. Fonts offer a subtle way for the reader to glean social and cultural meaning within the context of an infographic's story (Knight & Glaser, 2012; Kulahcioglu & de Melo, 2020). Similar to color, be aware that your audience might relate certain typographic treatments to certain emotions and situations based on how those typefaces have been used in other contexts (Brumberger, 2003). For example, typefaces similar to Abstract Groovy were commonly used during the 1960s and are still used today to conjure social or cultural associations with that time. Whereas typefaces like Desdemona (a high-waisted font) convey a cultural association to art deco or arts and crafts design styles, and Chalkboard invokes a handwritten, informal schoolhouse feel (Figure 6.14).

In addition to ascribing meaning to typefaces based on specific cultural or social contexts, audiences will recognize and gauge the match between the typeface and the text passage, such as using a "serious" typeface for a serious text passage (Brumberger, 2003). Likewise, audiences will be aware of the disconnect between typeface and the text passage. For example, consider the different typographic treatments applied to the phrase "data you can trust," and notice the interplay between treatment, meaning, and emotion (Figure 6.15). Which typographic treatment is most congruent with what is written? Which comes across as most trustworthy? Think about the qualities an audience might associate with trustworthy data—clean, methodical, straightforward, etc. When selecting fonts, you want to make intentional choices about typeface and treatments to ensure they are congruent with the meaning and affect you want to convey through the infographic.

Typeface, which refers to all characters (letters, numbers, punctuation) of the same design, is the first typographic treatment to select for your infographic. Common and often overused typeface examples include Times New Roman, Arial, and Calibri. Consider selecting typefaces different from what audiences typically see. One or two typefaces are adequate for an infographic because you can vary them by applying different font treatments. If selecting two typefaces, consider selecting one serif (has a small decorative stroke on the end of characters) and one sans serif (lacks a serif). Fonts should be easy to read, complementary, and harmonious. For example, the typefaces Trattatello and Chalkboard are so dissimilar they clash with each other, whereas the strikingness of Trattatello is more harmonious with a simple typeface such as Corbel, and Chalkboard is more harmonious with a complementary typeface such as Marker Felt (Table 6.1). Websites such as fontpair (fontpair.co) provide typography suggestions, pairings, and a generator to find a matching typeface to one you want to use.

In addition to typeface, font treatments such as bold, italics, underline, and all or small caps are other ways to emphasize and distinguish text in an infographic and increase readability (Song & Schwartz, 2008). However, there is no need to apply multiple treatments to the same text, such as ***bolding and italicizing*** words. One font treatment, **bold** or *italics*, is sufficient for adding emphasis while maintaining simplicity and clarity. Whether we are aware of it or not,

FIGURE 6.14 ■ Example Typefaces

ABSTRACT GROOVY

DESDEMONA

Chalkboard

FIGURE 6.15 ▦ Example of Incongruent and Congruent Relationships Between Typographic Treatments and Meaning

Data you can trust.

Data you can trust.

DATA YOU CAN TRUST.

𝕯ata you can trust.

Data you can trust.

TABLE 6.1 ▦ Examples of Font Pairings		
Clashing Font Pair	**Harmonious Font Pair**	**Harmonious Font Pair**
Trattello	*Trattello*	**Marker Felt**
Chalkboard	Corbel	Chalkboard

the brain is decoding and processing the font treatments to make sense of their interrelationship between their use and the rest of information on the page (Juni & Gross, 2008). Applying font treatments consistently throughout your infographic will help readers interpret and navigate your infographic more easily (Sundar et al., 2018).

Another way to vary fonts is to adjust type size. In an infographic, type sizes should vary based on the hierarchy of information (e.g., larger for main points or section headers, smaller for supporting details, visual labels, and sources). When working with typefaces and multiple font treatments, it is helpful to establish a font schema for elements of your infographic's story (Table 6.2). A schema reveals if your font typeface and treatment choices are congruent with your infographic's content and consistent across different infographic elements. You might refine the font schema during Step 8 of the development process, but establishing it in Step 6 ensures consist application as you begin drafting the infographic.

The following are considerations for creating a font schema for your infographic:

- Use no more than two typefaces for an infographic to maintain a clean overall appearance.

- If using two typefaces, select one serif and one sans serif typeface that complement rather than clash with each other, or use two complementary sans serif fonts for simplicity.

- Apply only one font treatment to a word, phrase, or sentence to add emphasis. Adding multiple font treatments (bolding, italicizing, and underlining) is another way of creating unnecessary visual clutter.

- Use font size as another way of representing the hierarchy and relative importance of information in an infographic.

TABLE 6.2 ■ Example Font Schema for Elements of an Infographic Story			
Infographic Story Elements	**Select Font Typeface**	**Apply Font Treatment**	**Adjust Font Size**
Title	Title (Palatino)	**Title (bold)**	**Title (28)**
Main points/Section header	Main points (Palatino)	**Main points (bold)**	**Main points (14)**
Secondary points	Secondary points (Avenir)	*Secondary points (italics)*	*Secondary points (12)*
Body text (introduction text, conclusion, supporting details)	Body (Avenir)	Body (regular)	Body (12)
Visual labels (e.g., chart values, icon descriptors, diagram labels)	Visual labels (Avenir)	Visual labels (regular)	Visual labels (10)
Sources	Sources (Palatino)	Sources (regular)	Sources (8)

CREATING FLOW

Flow shapes the audience's experience with the infographic's information. As with the concept of balance discussed in Step 4, flow is an infographic design element readers become aware of when its lacking. They will be aware when they get stuck on a piece of information that doesn't make sense or when they don't know where to direct their attention next. When an infographic flows, readers know right where to begin reading and their eyes navigate through the information with ease.

Individuals typically tend to exhibit left-to-right reading order in both print and online formats (Faraday, 2000). When first previewing information, such as in an infographic, readers tend to quickly scan an area to identify a point of entry or an anchor (Djamasbi et al., 2010). Therefore, it is important to use intentional visual cues to designate an entry point to the infographic and direct the audience's attention from that point to the next, acknowledging left-to-right reading preference. The simplest and most natural flow route, therefore, is an infographic that takes the audience through information presented left to right, top to bottom. If your layout uses a two-column design, for example, use visual cues to help readers flow through one column before reading the next.

An infographic with flow presents images, text, and sections with natural transitions from point to point. You can create flow using visual cues—such as headers, sub headers, dividers, shading, font size, and color changes—that help readers navigate through the infographic's story. Using visual cues organizes an infographic into digestible chunks that flow from one point to the next, thus helping the audience make sense of the infographic's story. The infographic, *Using CART Analysis to Inform Education Decisions*, applies several different visual cues to help readers flow through the infographic's information and visuals (Figure 6.16). Visual cues include using distinct and consistently formatted section headers that divide the infographic's content by key questions. Sections are further demarcated with different background colors. Within sections, dotted lines divide the content into further subsections. The white, oval-shaped background encompassing the target icon in the upper section gives visual emphasis to the information it contains. As you can see, the infographic uses a left-to-right,

FIGURE 6.16 ■ Use of Visual Cues to Create Flow

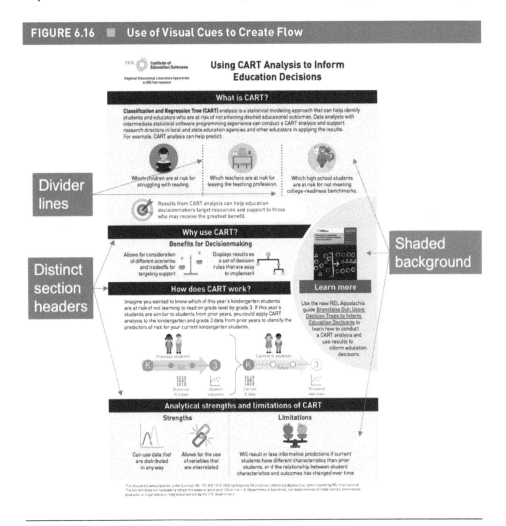

Source: U.S. Department of Education, 2021

top-to-bottom layout with the exception of the call-to-action section, which anchors to the right side of the infographic. Using a semicircular shaped section with a background shaded in a different color, the design signals to readers that this section stands apart from the rest of the information.

The following are considerations for creating flow in your infographic:

- Be intentional about the infographic's point of entry, knowing that the audience might tend to read left to right, top to bottom from that point.

- If the infographic incorporates a less common navigation route for its information, be sure to use clear and consistent visual cues to signal each transition in the visual pathway.

- Use visual cues, such as section headers, divider lines, and background shading, to designate sections and cluster digestible chunks of information in the infographic.

DETERMINING THE FOCAL POINT

Infographics pack a visual punch when they draw readers' attention to a focal point that connects to the infographic's central message or topic. The focal point is what readers automatically see when they first view the infographic, and it can immediately engage the audience. Therefore, the focal point should be compelling, engaging, and visually appealing.

People tend to scan information for a visual anchor and then read the text next to that anchor (Djamasbi et al., 2010; Faraday, 2000). When connected to the text in a purposeful way, the visual focal point also helps readers comprehend the meaning of the text faster. For example, our infographic, *When School Employees Cross the Line*, uses two large, color-saturated silhouettes populated with characteristics of school employee sexual misconduct offenders and student victims to attract the audience's attention (Figure 6.17). With the placement of data within the focal point, the reader can more easily associate and recall the characteristics of offenders and victims than if the infographic emphasized a different focal point or no focal point at all. We then use the title and schoolhouse icon in black to pull the eyes to the top of the infographic and designate the entry point for reading the rest of the content top to bottom.

Overuse of visuals and color saturation can result in an infographic with visual elements that compete for readers' attention. Too many competing visuals can obscure the entry point and navigation pathway of the infographic, leaving readers unsure of where to focus their attention and how to navigate the infographic. In a matter of minutes, this can create confusion and cloud the central message of your infographic's story. The infographic, *Building Bridges for Girls in Engineering*, demonstrates how photos, enlarged icons, and saturations of dark colors can overwhelm an infographic with visual elements that compete for readers' immediate attention (Figure 6.18). When you look at the infographic, where do your eyes first land? On one of the photographs, the bridge with walking people icons, the bar chart, or a number? Where does it go next? The answer is probably different for different people, which affirms that the infographic lacks an intentional focal point. Consequently, the central message of the infographic's story may be unclear to readers, given the visual emphasis of multiple data elements. The focal point of the infographic could be improved by revisiting the

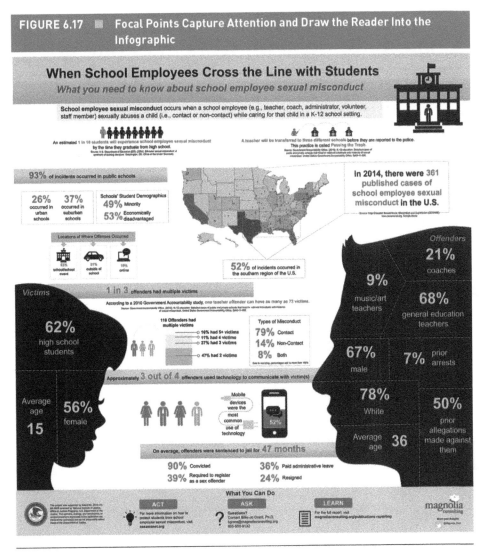

FIGURE 6.17 ■ Focal Points Capture Attention and Draw the Reader Into the Infographic

Source: Stephanie Wilkerson, Anne Cosby, Molly Henschel, Billie-Jo Grant, 2017

storyline in Step 3 to see if it could be simpler (e.g., the bar chart ratings may not be integral to the central message and could be eliminated). Designers could also reconsider the visual representations in Step 4 (e.g., bridge image, photos, icons), reevaluate the application of color saturations, and remove any visuals that are distracting and don't directly support a main point (e.g., the walking person icons).

Being intentional about an infographic's focal point ensures you direct the reader's attention purposefully. Avoid making the focal point a logo, supporting detail of the infographic, or anything that might overshadow the central message. A focal point doesn't need to be large or the largest visual on the page. Smaller focal points like photographs or images with concentrated color will also draw the eye's attention (Malamed, 2009).

FIGURE 6.18 ■ Too Many Focal Points Can Confuse the Reader

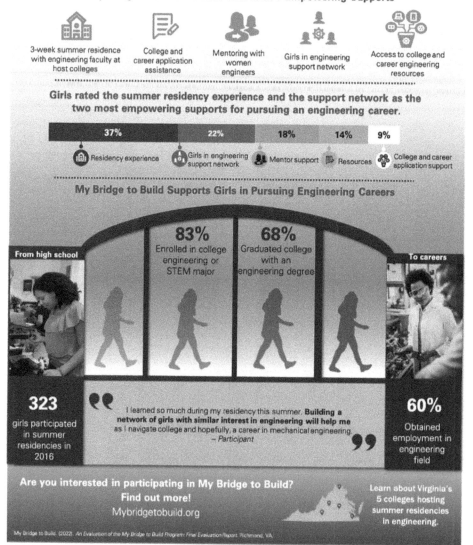

Building Bridges for Girls in Engineering

My Bridge to Build is a Virginia-based program that supports rising senior high school girls in enrolling in and graduating from college engineering programs and obtaining employment in engineering fields.

My Bridge to Build Provides Girls with 5 Empowering Supports

3-week summer residence with engineering faculty at host colleges

College and career application assistance

Mentoring with women engineers

Girls in engineering support network

Access to college and career engineering resources

Girls rated the summer residency experience and the support network as the two most empowering supports for pursuing an engineering career.

| 37% | 22% | 18% | 14% | 9% |

Residency experience Girls in engineering support network Mentor support Resources College and career application support

My Bridge to Build Supports Girls in Pursuing Engineering Careers

From high school

83% Enrolled in college engineering or STEM major

68% Graduated college with an engineering degree

To careers

323 girls participated in summer residencies in 2016

"I learned so much during my residency this summer. **Building a network of girls with similar interest in engineering will help me** as I navigate college and hopefully, a career in mechanical engineering." – Participant

60% Obtained employment in engineering field

Are you interested in participating in My Bridge to Build? Find out more! Mybridgetobuild.org

Learn about Virginia's 5 colleges hosting summer residencies in engineering.

My Bridge to Build. (2022). *An Evaluation of the My Bridge to Build Program: Final Evaluation Report.* Richmond, VA.

Source: Stephanie Wilkerson and Anne Cosby, 2023

A focal point emerges from an infographic's story and can attract readers through intentional design elements such as layout, size, color, or type of visual (e.g., photograph, data visualization, icon, illustration). To determine an infographic's focal point, revisit the visuals and data identified in Step 4. Think about which one best represents the central message in a compelling and engaging way. You can factor the focal point into the infographic's layout design in Step 5 and play with where it ultimately resides when you begin drafting the infographic in Steps 7 and 8.

Does every infographic need a focal point? Not necessarily, but an infographic is more powerful when a visual element captures the audience's attention and connects to the infographic's story. Be aware that something in your infographic will immediately attract the eye no matter what, so be intentional about where you want to direct readers' attention and for what purpose.

The following are considerations for incorporating a focal point into your infographic:

- Be intentional about where you want to draw readers' eyes using a focal point that supports the infographic's story.

- Be aware of how multiple, dominant visual elements may compete for the audience's attention and either simplify or minimize visual emphasis to elevate one visual as the focal point.

BOX 6.4. STEP 6 DESIGN CHALLENGE

DESIGN CHALLENGE: WHAT IF I'M UNSURE WHAT AN INFOGRAPHIC'S AUDIENCE WILL ASSOCIATE WITH AN INFOGRAPHIC'S COLOR CHOICES?

Sometimes it will be difficult to anticipate the associations your audience might make with colors. Your audience might be the general public or other broadly defined population representing a variety of cultures, religions, and social backgrounds. You might not have an immediate connection or access to your audience, such as parents, organizational leaders, policymakers, or people living in a different country. Nevertheless, *what can you do to inform yourself about what color associations might be relevant and important to my audience*?

Ask your audience in Step 1. As covered in Step 1, *Identify Your Audience*, you want to learn as much as possible about your intended audience for the infographic. This includes asking questions about their background and any associations they might have with colors and images. You want to assess if there are any colors to avoid because of a negative association, or colors you might want to include because of a positive association. Often your client or others who interact directly with the audience for the infographic will have sufficient knowledge to provide this input. If you can contact representatives of your audience, then running potential color combinations by them during early steps of infographic development is optimal.

Do your research. If you are unable to ask someone directly about potential color associations, then conduct some research. There are many online articles, blogs, and research studies as well as books about the meaning and symbolism of colors.

Clarify what role you want color to play. As described in this chapter, color can evoke several associations for your audience, so it's important to be clear about how prominently you want to use it as a design element in your infographic.

Seek reviewer input in Step 9. In Step 9, *Review the Infographic*, you want to invite as many people representing your audience to review the draft infographic before finalization. This is an opportunity to collect feedback from your audience about how they perceive and experience the use of color in your infographic. Even if an audience has strong associations with colors in a particular social, cultural, or religious context, they might not make the same associations in your infographic based on how you've applied color to the infographic's visual elements. Seeking your audience's input at this stage of development helps to ensure the audience interprets the meaning of colors the way you intend.

BOX 6.5. PLANETS ILLUSTRATIVE EXAMPLE—CHOOSE DESIGN ELEMENTS

In Step 5, *Select Layout*, we drafted a layout for the PLANETS infographic with sections for the title and introduction, main points, supporting details, and conclusion. Now in Step 6 we select the design elements of color, font, flow, and focal point.

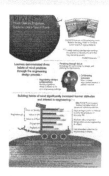

Source: Stephanie Wilkerson and Anne Cosby, 2023

We started with the PLANETS logo, which we identified in Step 4, *Identify Data and Visuals*, to consider branding colors. The project has two logos, one with a night sky background and one with dark blue font treatment and an array of accent colors. Because the PLANETS program focuses on planetary science, and more specifically Mars, we also wanted to consider a color palette that people would associate with space and the planet Mars. During our process of identifying possible visuals in Step 4, we found space imagery that we might incorporate into different sections of the infographic, including a photograph of Mars for the introduction section. Between the project logo and the Mars photograph, we had a good basis for our color palette. Next, we uploaded the logos and Mars photograph to Coolors.co to get HEX codes to narrow our color choices for the infographic. We ended up using the dark blue and turquoise from the PLANETS logo, a brownish orange from the Mars photograph, and a lighter shade of turquoise for the background color (Table 6.3). We drafted a color hierarchy as we considered how we might apply these colors to the infographic's visual elements. We

TABLE 6.3 ■ PLANETS Infographic Color Palette and Applications			
● Icons	● Mars photograph	● Data visualization	● Background
● Data visualization	● Subheaders	● Accents	
● Main points	● Supporting details		
● Supporting details			

then tested our color contrasts using WebAIM and determined that the dark blue text on the light blue background had sufficient contrasts. The original color we selected from the Mars photograph did not have sufficient contrast, so we had to darken the color until it passed the contrast text. Next, we printed our palette in black and white and determined that color gradations across the four colors were discernible when printed in gray scale.

Next we selected font typeface, treatment, and size for the PLANETS infographics. To keep the design elements simple, we selected one typeface, Avenir, for the entirety of the infographic except for the sources, which we selected Futura in 8-point font. We then drafted a font hierarchy by applying font treatments, including color, bold, italics, and font size (Table 6.4). We knew this might change as we moved into the construction phase of the infographic in Step 8, but establishing the hierarchy in the design phase helped us to establish consistency and harmony.

TABLE 6.4 ▪ PLANETS Infographic Font Schema			
Infographic Story Elements	**Font Typeface**	**Font Treatment**	**Font Size**
Title	Avenir	Avenir (white font color)	**Avenir** **(18 point)**
Main points/Section header		**Avenir** (indigo, **bold**)	**Avenir** **(16 point)**
Secondary points		Avenir (brown)	Avenir (12 point)
Body text (introduction text, conclusion, supporting details)		*Avenir* (indigo, *italics*)	Avenir (12 point)
Visual labels (e.g., chart values, icon descriptors, diagram labels)		Avenir (brown)	Avenir (12 point)
Sources	Futura	Futura (color)	Futura (8 point)

For flow and focal point, we knew we wanted to work in elements of the Mars photograph, but at this stage in the design, we weren't entirely sure to what extent. We also knew we wanted to incorporate a data visualization using a caricature of the Mars rover to represent one main point and an illustration using icons to represent a second main point. We realized we had potentially three competing visuals for a focal point. Given this, we thought we might use the Mars photo image as background for the introduction, thereby establishing it as the focal point, or at the very least using it as a powerful visual cue to draw readers' eyes to the introduction. We thought dotted lines would work well as section dividers between the introductory text and each of the main points. We envisioned using font size and background colors as visual cues to minimize emphasis of the sources at the bottom of the page. With our selected visuals, layout, and design elements identified, we were ready to sketch the PLANETS infographic in Step 7.

NOW IT'S YOUR TURN!

- Find and review WebFX's "Psychology of Color Infographic"[1] (2022) and consider the following:
  - How is the psychology of color in branding and marketing also relevant to applying color in infographics intended for other communication purposes, such as presenting study results?
  - What visual cues and design elements does the infographic use to divide content into sections and facilitate how the audience reads through the infographic's content with ease?
  - How does the infographic apply a consistent schema of color and font treatments to the text and icons?
- Create a font schema for your infographic using Table 6.5.

TABLE 6.5 ■ Create a Font Schema for Your Infographic			
Infographic Story Elements	**Font Typeface**	**Font Treatment**	**Font Size**
Title			
Main points/Section header			
Secondary points			
Body text (introduction text, conclusion, supporting details)			
Visual labels (e.g., chart values, icon descriptors, diagram labels)			
Sources			

RESOURCES

Check it out!

Font and typography resources:

- dafont: https://www.dafont.com/
- Fontsquirrel: https://www.fontsquirrel.com/
- fontpair (font books, tools, games, and websites): https://www.fontpair.co/resources

Color resources:

- Infographics about selecting colors based on their associations: https://louisem.com/222511/business-colors

- Coolors.com: https://coolors.co/

- Adobe Color: https://color.adobe.com/create/color-wheel

- ColorBrewer 2.0: https://colorbrewer2.org/#type=sequential&scheme=BuGn&n=3

IES Graphic Design for Researchers: https://drive.google.com/file/d/1MsKjsIkuIdhPh8pBwE3-hQPOx5O-36Mp/view

NOTE

1. https://www.webfx.com/blog/web-design/psychology-of-color-infographic/

STEP 7: SKETCH YOUR IDEAS

LEARNING OBJECTIVES

In Step 7, you will learn

- the importance of sketching your infographic before digitally constructing it, and

- ways to use the sketching process to play with the layout, white space, focal point, and balance of an infographic.

The tendency at this stage in the infographic development process might be to skip to constructing your infographic digitally, but first sketching design ideas on paper in Step 7 can save you time in the long run. While perhaps a seemingly simplistic step in the development process, sketching design ideas allows you to merge design decisions from all prior steps before committing them to a digital format. With sketching you can test how well the visuals you identified in Step 4 merge with the layout, white space, focal point, and balance you designed in Steps 5 and 6. Using simple pencil-and-paper sketches, you can toy with the layout, vary placement of visuals, and try out different ways of organizing information on the page without the labor of digital design. Sketches will also help you see if the volume of information and story components you identified in Step 3 will fit on the page. This process will help you determine if you need to reduce information, revise your infographic story, or eliminate visual clutter that doesn't support the infographic's purpose.

A sketch is also an effective way of helping others, such as collaborators and clients, conceptualize the audience interface with the infographic and provide feedback during the pre-production stage before you invest time in digital production. Sharing a sketch of your infographic will also help ensure your design collaborators, clients, or any other decision makers understand the vision for communicating a visual story through the infographic. The sketch becomes a springboard for discussions about what the infographic should or shouldn't include based on information priorities and the infographic's purpose you identified in Step 2. These conversations can also help cultivate a shared understanding and vision for how to visually represent the infographic's story elements to convey its main points and message. Engaging collaborators and clients in providing input during this step in the planning process can help mitigate any dissatisfaction with the final result down the line.

The sketching process simplifies the infographic to render an initial testing of your design ideas. There is no need to draw every detail or even use color in the sketch. You want to include enough visual detail to get an idea of how your visuals and layout will come together. If drawing isn't your strong suit, you can represent visuals as shaded boxes or shapes to show their relative size and placement in the layout (see PLANETS Illustrative Example—Step 5 Layout to Step 7 Basic Sketch). In its simplicity, the sketch portrays a static version of an infographic and does not capture any interactive elements, such as video or animation.

The layout you selected in Step 5 serves as your guide and starting point for the sketching process. Depending on the complexity of your infographic, you might begin with a basic sketch that captures the key sections or elements of your story as depicted in your Step 5 layout (see PLANETS Illustrative Example—Step 5 Layout to Step 7 Basic Sketch). Starting with a basic sketch for an infographic is similar to creating an outline for a report. It might include a simple rendering of your main visuals, bracketed placeholders for text, shapes or boxes for icons or photographs, and section demarcations for key story elements including title, introduction, main points, conclusion, and sources. Beginning with a basic sketch can help you determine how and if your planned content and visuals fit on the page. Use as many pages as necessary to represent the length and orientation of your infographic, keeping in mind the size parameters you established for the infographic in Step 5.

BOX 7.1. PLANETS ILLUSTRATIVE EXAMPLE—STEP 5 LAYOUT TO STEP 7 BASIC SKETCH

In Step 5, we created a layout for the PLANETS infographic based on the sections of our story elements—title, introduction, two main points with supporting details, conclusion, and sources (Figure 7.1). We also determined in Step 5 that the infographic should be suitable for printing on a single page, so we used one sheet of paper for sketching. Working from our layout, we spent about five minutes sketching the four basic sections for our story elements:

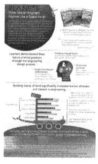

Source: Stephanie Wilkerson and Anne Cosby, 2023

- **Title and introduction.** We envisioned using part of a Mars image we identified in Step 4 as the background for our title and introduction section. We sketched an outline of what it might look like to demarcate the section.
- **First main point.** We planned on using various icons to represent our first main point with one larger icon connecting to three smaller icons with supporting details. Based on our layout, the visual would be to the left of a text box that would state the main point. We used circles and brackets to designate where the icons and text boxes would go.
- **Second main point.** Our vision for the second main point was to create a rendering of the Mars rover the PLANETS project used as a mascot, Rosie, in their curriculum materials and merge the rover with a bar chart. We added a rough sketch of what that might look like and added brackets to designate a text box for a statement about

---

FIGURE 7.1   ■   From Step 5 Layout to Step 7 Basic Sketch

STEP 5 Layout   STEP 7 Basic Sketch

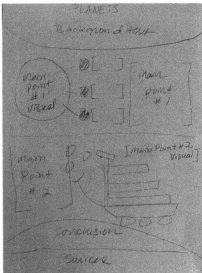

STEP 5 Layout
TITLE   Introduction and   Program Background
MAIN POINT 1 VISUAL   Supporting Details   Main Point 1   Statement
Main Point 2   Statement   **MAIN POINT 2 VISUAL**   Supporting Details
CONCLUSION   Call-to-action and   Sources

the main point. With the basic sketch, it was clear we would not have sufficient space for additional data and visuals we had identified in Steps 3 and 4 to support this main point. We determined that omitting it from the infographic's story would not weaken the central message, and the infographic could still achieve its purpose without it. We therefore omitted the supporting detail from our design plan. Had we skipped the sketching process and jumped to digital production, we would have wasted time creating the visual and trying to get it to work on the page. Instead, a five-minute basic sketch allowed us to determine if our content would fit.

- **Conclusion and sources.** At the bottom of the page, we played with the idea of using the Mars image again as the ground for the Mars rover visual and transition point for the conclusion. We sketched the outline of where we would place the photo, similar to the top introduction section.

If your infographic's design includes sophisticated visuals and several detailed story elements, starting with a basic sketch and progressing to one with more detail allows you to test additional design elements. By adding more detail to the next iterative sketch, you can focus on the interplay between text and visuals, image placement, relative size, and white space (see PLANETS Illustrative Example—Sketch With More Detail). You can get a general idea of what will attract the reader's attention through visual size and color saturation, shown with pencil shading. Sketching visual details also helps you identify extraneous visuals that might clutter the infographic, thereby distracting the reader, interrupting visual flow, and diminishing white space. Visual white space reduces the cognitive demand on the brain to comprehend and process information and helps prevent your audience from becoming overloaded with information (Coates, 2014). Think of white space as a mental pause for the brain to momentarily rest before moving onto the next piece of information.

BOX 7.2. PLANETS ILLUSTRATIVE EXAMPLE— SKETCH WITH MORE DETAIL

By adding more detail to the PLANETS infographic sketch, we could test our design for the use of white space and balance within and across sections. We could also approximate the relative size of main visuals and determine if the focal point we wanted was in fact what would draw the reader's attention compared to other main visuals. This rendering did not include every detail, such as text for the introduction, supporting details, or conclusion. Rather, it focused mostly on the main points and the use of space through the following (Figure 7.2):

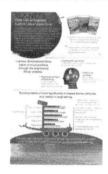

● **Sketching main visuals.** Instead of placeholders for the main visuals in the basic sketch, we sketched them in more detail. This included adding an outline of the main silhouette icon

Source: Stephanie Wilkerson and Anne Cosby, 2023

FIGURE 7.2 ■ **Sketch With More Detail**

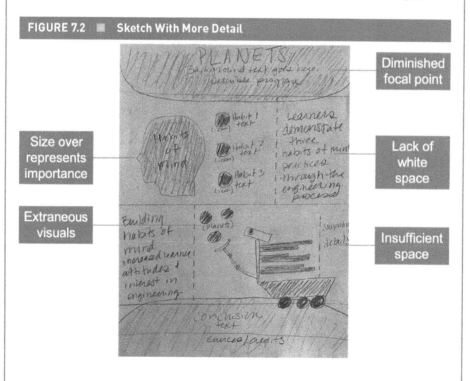

selected in Step 4 to represent the "habits of mind concept" and three shaded circles to represent the icons for each habits of mind practices. The practice icons were too detailed to sketch for our drawing ability, but the point at this stage was to gauge how their color saturation might attract or detract attention from the main visuals. With this in mind, we shaded the other visual elements in the infographic that we knew would be filled with color.

- **Adding text for main points.** We next added the main-point statements we drafted in Step 3 because we wanted to clearly emphasize the key takeaway from each visual. While consistent with the basic sketch from our layout, adding the text made it clear that we did not want the audience to start reading on the right side of the page, when we know the natural tendency is to read left to right. We concluded that placing the main-point statement to the right of the main visual inhibited the flow of the infographic, and we would change it in the next sketch iteration.

- **Reviewing for visual balance and focal point.** After adding some details and shading to the infographic's main visuals, we could easily see that the habits of mind silhouette icon was too big. It did not include enough meaningful information to warrant its size, particularly relative to the other main visuals. We planned on the Mars photo being the focal point to draw the reader's attention to the top of the page and introduction, but this sketch helped us see that it was competing with our other visuals and would need to change.

- **Reviewing for white space.** With the sketch populated with key visual elements, it was clear there was insufficient room for supporting details in some sections and a lack of white space throughout the design. Even in this sketch phase, we could pinpoint cluttered areas and extraneous visuals, such as the small planets (shaded circles in the sketch) Rosie the Mars rover was juggling. While connecting with the planetary science theme, their inclusion did not add value to communicating the main points, so we decided to remove them in the next sketch iteration. We could also see the space was insufficient for some of the background information we identified in Step 4.

Creating an infographic will take several iterations to move from idea to final product, so starting with a sketch, or multiple sketches, decreases time making substantive edits and changes in digital format. In under an hour, you can develop a series of iterative sketches that test which design ideas will work, need revising, or should be eliminated (see PLANETS Illustrative Example—Sketch of Modified Layout).

The following are considerations for sketching detail in an infographic:

- As you sketch, keep in mind the audience, purpose, and story for your infographic and the design considerations covered in Steps 4 through 6.

- Take what you learn from sketching and keep iterating on the design. Try sketching different ways of displaying data and other visuals with an eye for creating balance, flow, and white space, both within and across sections.

- Even at this stage in the development process you can begin identifying and eliminating anything unnecessary.

BOX 7.3. PLANETS ILLUSTRATIVE EXAMPLE—SKETCH OF MODIFIED LAYOUT

Based on what we learned from previous sketches of the PLANETS infographic, we knew we needed to make some changes to our layout. In the next iteration, we wanted to create room for a few more details as well as white space. We wanted to adjust the placement and sizing of our focal point and two other main visuals to improve balance and flow. We wanted the placement and relative size of our main visuals to make it clear to the reader how to navigate through the infographic. To accomplish our objectives, we changed the following in the next iteration of our sketch (Figure 7.3):

Source: Stephanie Wilkerson and Anne Cosby, 2023

- **Removing extraneous visuals.** We removed the planets Rosie the rover was juggling to allow for more white space and create room for supporting details.
- **Adjusting focal point.** To draw the reader's eye to the introduction, we repositioned and enlarged the Mars image. Although we knew the audience might notice the other main visuals at first glance, the larger size and color saturation of the Mars photo in the upper left corner would signal the infographic's entry point.
- **Adjusting for balance, flow, and white space.** With the entry point in the upper left corner, we repositioned the other two main visuals in a zig-zag formation to support navigating through the infographic from left to right and top to bottom. This would improve balance among the three main visuals and help with flow through the infographic. We

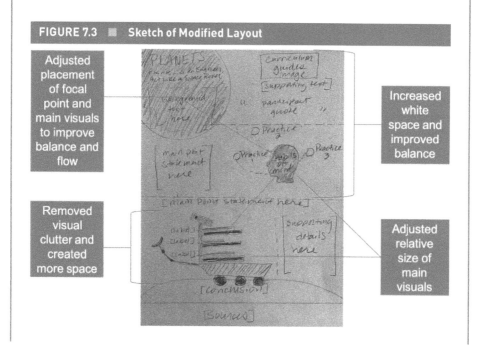

FIGURE 7.3 ■ Sketch of Modified Layout

Adjusted placement of focal point and main visuals to improve balance and flow

Increased white space and improved balance

Removed visual clutter and created more space

Adjusted relative size of main visuals

also reduced the size of the two main visuals to create more white space and room for supporting details. For the habits of mind visual, we adjusted its balance by circling the three icons around the central silhouette icon instead of listing them to the right of it. We thought this would also create more coherence for the visual overall.

Once you arrive at a sketch that incorporates your main story and visual elements, you are ready to move into digital production. The completion of Step 7 is the last step of design planning, and while there are several steps involved in creating a design plan, it likely only accounts for 30% to 40% of the time you will invest in creating an infographic. You will continue to test and revise aspects of your design and visuals as you bring them to life digitally. Elements you did not test or manipulate with sketching, such as color, font treatment, and interactive features, will surface new considerations for the design. Some ideas that worked on paper might not work as well as once digitized. Ideas you could capture in a simple drawing might be more complex to execute. Regardless, the sketching process is an important step that reveals some design flaws and necessary adjustments that will save time during production.

BOX 7.4. STEP 7 DESIGN CHALLENGE

DESIGN CHALLENGE: WHAT IF MY DESIGN DOESN'T SEEM FEASIBLE ONCE SKETCHED?

The sketching process might reveal challenging aspects of your design you had not considered up to this point. You might struggle with fitting extensive amounts of information on the page, or you might find that your creative vision is more complex or elaborate than what you thought. *What do you do when your vision isn't coming together as you had hoped in a sketch?*

Go back to the basics. If you are getting lost in the details or the sketch is looking too complicated, strip it down to the basic elements. Rather than draw the complex details of visuals, use outlines, boxes, or shapes to estimate their size and placement. With this approach, see if your main visuals and designated sections for each story element fit on the page. If not, consider revising your layout before adding more detail. If everything fits and appears balanced, then save the production of complex visual details for Step 8.

Eliminate nonessential details. Revisit the content of your story you outlined in Step 3. Clarify what information is germane to the story, and be willing to let go of information that, while interesting, doesn't directly serve the infographic's main purpose.

Use clickable features to annex information. If eliminating details is problematic, use hyperlinks to ancillary documents or popups that contain relevant information. These won't consume space on the page.

Consider resizing the infographic. If you eliminated everything you could and considered clickable features, but are still pressed for space, try lengthening the infographic. Even an inch can make a world of difference in your design without drastically changing its size or its presentation on a printed page.

NOW IT'S YOUR TURN!

- Find an infographic online (for example, visit Love Infographics at https://lovefreeinfographics.wordpress.com/) and try drawing a basic sketch of it, using lines, boxes, circles, etc. While this is reverse of the actual design process, the activity will help you dissect and sketch the basic elements of an infographic.
  - Could you easily discern and draw the sections of the infographic?
  - In looking at the placement of main visuals, are they balanced on the page?
  - Were you able to account for white space in the infographic?
  - Is there anything you would change in the infographic based on what you learned from sketching it?

- Sketch your infographic! Start with the layout and sizing considerations from Step 5, and grab paper, pencil, and a good eraser. If your layout follows the rule of thirds, consider using graph paper or draw gridlines on blank paper to divide it in thirds. Drawing section dividers according to your design will also help with placing, sizing, and balancing your main visuals. Make sure you give some representation, even if just placeholder brackets, for each story element (title, introduction, main points, supporting details, conclusion, and sources). Try starting with a basic sketch and progress to a more detailed version. With each change or iteration, make sure the infographic remains aligned with its purpose and central message.

RESOURCES

Check it out!

- 12 Visual Hierarchy Principles Every Non-Designer Needs to Know: https://visme.co/blog/visual-hierarchy/#visual-hierarchy-infographic

STEP 8: DRAFT THE INFOGRAPHIC

LEARNING OBJECTIVES

In Step 8, you will learn how to

- select a design platform based on your ability, resources, and collaboration requirements;

- access user-friendly design tools and resources, many of which are free;

- develop and apply design elements from Step 6 to images, icons, shapes, and data visualizations;

- create the foundation for your infographic based on the selected layout in Step 5;

- layer in visuals and text based on your sketch from Step 7; and

- make sure your infographic is 508 compliant.

Up to this point, you've planned your infographic's design including identifying your audience, purpose, and story; creating a layout; selecting visual design elements; and sketching your infographic vision. In Step 8, you shift from planning to production and bring your infographic to life. Moving from an infographic sketch to a digital format reveals how well the design elements you chose in Steps 4 through 7 work together to communicate the compelling story you created in Steps 1 through 3.

Infographic production begins with selecting an online template or software program to create your infographic and weighing the pros and cons of each. Next, you download or develop the infographic visuals you identified in Step 4, format and size them, and apply color and font treatments from Step 6. You then build the infographic's foundation by constructing the background, sections, and section dividers based on Step 5's layout and Step 7's draft sketches. Next, you layer the visuals and text onto your infographic's foundation. Lastly, you will ensure your infographic is accessible for people with disabilities. This chapter demonstrates these steps in the production process.

SELECTING A DESIGN PLATFORM

Production begins with selecting the platform for building your infographic. There are two main platform options, software programs or online templates, each having pros and cons to consider. The main consideration is whether you want maximum customizability using a software program or if you prefer online templates that come with ready-made, but modifiable, design elements. Deciding which platform is most appropriate for you will depend on your learning curve with using the platform, skill level in creating visuals, need for customization, collaboration requirements, and budget (see Considerations for Selecting a Design Platform).

BOX 8.1. CONSIDERATIONS FOR SELECTING A DESIGN PLATFORM

- Will the platform (software program or online template) require you to learn how to use it or are you already familiar with it?
- Does the platform come with built-in templates and visual elements—such as icons, images, shapes, and modifiable data visualizations—and can you create and import your own visuals?
- Does the platform allow you to customize your infographic in the manner you need (e.g., layout, color and font selection, visual creation)?
- Does the platform offer collaboration features for sharing and editing the infographic with others? In what file format can you export the infographic?

Each design platform has supports and limitations to consider. We prefer PowerPoint as a user-friendly and widely-known software program for creating infographics. You can also search online for free, downloadable infographic templates in PowerPoint. More skilled designers might prefer graphic design programs like Inkscape or Adobe Illustrator for maximum customization. Websites, such as Canva, Venngage, and Piktochart, specialize in infographic templates with built-in and modifiable design elements, such as backgrounds, layouts, color and font schemes, visualizations, and text boxes. When exploring this option, consider how well an online template aligns with the design plan you developed in Steps 1 through 7. While you might think an online template will save time, the platform's limitations could require time-consuming design modifications, "work arounds," and compromises. These websites offer free templates with account registration and more features with a paid account, so determine what features you need before you commit to using a template. We recommend taking time to consider the features of online infographic template websites, Microsoft PowerPoint, and graphic design programs to inform your selection of the platform and program that is right for you (Table 8.1).

TABLE 8.1 ■ Considerations for Selecting a Design Platform			
Considerations	**Online Infographic Templates** (e.g., Canva, Piktochart, Venngage)	**Microsoft PowerPoint**	**Graphic design programs (e.g., Inkscape, Adobe Illustrator)**
Templates and built-in visual elements	● Ready-to-go infographic templates, including options for different layouts (e.g., timeline, sequential, and categorical) and styles. Pick the one that most closely aligns with your planned design and modify. ● Include limited libraries of visual elements such as icons, illustrations, and photos. ● Can upload visuals, but can't edit once uploaded. ● Offer editable templates for charts and graphs, but not as customizable as Excel. Some include applications, such as Flourish, that allow more customization of charts and graphs.	● No built-in infographic templates, but free, downloadable PowerPoint templates are available online. ● Office 365 provides built-in icons, and extensions from websites such as the Noun Project allow easy icon access. ● Can create or insert visual elements and image files. ● Can fully customize charts and graphs with Excel compatibility.	● No templates. ● Need to create or insert all visual elements.
Customization	● Moderately customizable with color and limited font changes, and replaceable icons and images. ● Potentially time consuming to change each individual element of an infographic template. ● "Blank" infographic template available for customization.	● Fully customizable. ● No creative restrictions for infographic. ● Development of design ideas limited only by skill level and technical ability.	● Fully customizable. ● No creative restrictions for infographic. ● Development of design ideas limited only by skill level and technical ability.

(Continued)

	Online Infographic Templates (e.g., Canva, Piktochart, Venngage)	Microsoft PowerPoint	Graphic design programs (e.g., Inkscape, Adobe Illustrator)
TABLE 8.1 ■ **Considerations for Selecting a Design Platform (*Continued*)**			
Considerations			
Sharing and editing capabilities	• Sharing and collaboration abilities may have restrictions. Explore options. • Depending free or paid account, infographics are downloadable as an image or PDF file.	• Easy to share and edit files as needed. • Files can be saved as images and PDFs for dissemination.	• Requires software access to open and edit files. • Files can be saved as images and PDFs for dissemination.
Skill level	• Friendly for beginners.	• Friendly for beginners. • Slight learning curve for making visuals using basic techniques.	• Advanced, requires training. • Steep learning curve that can be time intensive for using sophisticated tools.
Cost	• Free accounts available. • Certain features only available with paid account.	• Readily available for most users, and free if you already have the Microsoft Office suite.	• Inkscape is a free software. Other graphic design programs can be expensive.

The following are considerations for selecting an infographic platform:

• Select the platform and program that best support the design elements of your infographic story. While creatively inspirating, avoid letting online templates derail you from your carefully planned infographic design. The story drives the design, not the other way around.

• Online templates come with some visual design advantages if you're just starting out, but could require more time than anticipated if the template requires extensive modifications to adhere to your design plan. Be mindful of an online template's design limitations before committing to it.

• If you start in an online template, but want to make further edits in PowerPoint, download it as a PDF and use Adobe Acrobat Pro to convert it to a PPT file. It might not convert perfectly, so formatting glitches once in PowerPoint will need addressing.

• If you are working with collaborators on production using an online template, you may need to upgrade to a paid account to share editing capabilities. Check costs before committing to an online platform.

- Creating an infographic in PowerPoint may be easier than you think. With basic technical skills in an already familiar platform, access to high-quality visuals, and your design plan, you can bring your infographic story to life.

The following sections demonstrate how to build an infographic using the PLANETS example in PowerPoint. PowerPoint is an optimal platform for demonstrating the step-by-step production process from beginning to end, including building a layout, developing visuals, and applying design elements throughout the infographic. The following sections demonstrate three building essentials for creating infographics, regardless of platform:

I. Developing and formatting visuals according your design plan

II. Creating the foundation of your infographic, including the background, sections, and visual cues

III. Layering in your visuals and text

BUILDING ESSENTIALS: DEVELOPING AND FORMATTING VISUALS

Once you determine the design platform for your infographic, you will access or develop the visuals you identified in Step 4. This process involves selecting the appropriate file type for the visuals you will insert into your infographic. In working with images, icons, shapes, and data visualizations you will also apply your color and font choices from Step 6. The formatting of visuals according to your design plan ensures that all images in an infographic—photographs, icons, illustrations, data displays—are of high quality and consistent in appearance. Because an infographic's visuals are the main storyteller, they need to fully incorporate the design elements of the overall infographic, regardless of the platform you select for production.

Selecting File Type for Visuals

Whether you construct your infographic in PowerPoint, an online template, or other software program, the production process requires understanding the different file types for working with visuals. There are many file types for icons, illustrations, and other images, but the most common types are raster images (JPEG and PNG) and vector images (SVG), each containing data about an image's attributes, such as color.

- *Raster image file types*: Raster image files display static images where every pixel has a defined color arranged in grid to represent an image. Generally, the more pixels when printed on a page, the higher the resolution and sharper the image quality. JPEG and PNG images are raster image formats and are the most common file types for creating static infographics.
  - ○ **JPEG** file types are compressed, which makes them ideal for storing photographs at smaller sizes. If you are using a photograph in your infographic, save it as a JPEG file. This format displays a high-quality image, while reducing the space and

bandwidth needed to load your infographic digitally. JPEG images do not have transparent backgrounds, so when you layer them over a colored background, the audience will see a white box around it (Figure 8.1).

○ **PNG** file types are ideal for storing files with fewer colors than photographs, such as icons and illustrations. PNG file types support transparent backgrounds, so you can layer them onto colored backgrounds in your infographic.

● *Vector image file types*: These image types can be resized and edited using graphic design software programs, such as Adobe Illustrator or Inkscape. Vector images store image attributes in formulas or equations, rather than pixels in raster images. Because they are resolution independent, unlike raster images, they are ideal for website images or logos where the size may be scaled up or down to accommodate a wide range of viewing devices without compromising image quality.

FIGURE 8.1 ■ JPEG vs PNG File Types on a Colored Background

PLANETS Logo File Types

JPEG Image

White background

PNG Image

Transparent background

Working With Images

If you decided to use a photograph or illustration in your infographic in Step 4, search for images on stock photo and image websites, such as iStock, Unsplash, or Pixabay. Avoid searching Google for images—image quality varies and you could violate license requirements (see section on licensing requirements in Step 4). When searching images on stock photo and image websites, you can filter your search by license type (e.g., creative or editorial), layout orientation (e.g., horizontal, vertical, square), number of people, and ethnicity (see Design Resource How To: Colorizing and Downloading Images With iStock). You can also enter a HEX code from a color in your design palette to search for images. Using this feature to search and download images creates continuity across your infographic's visual elements. Account subscriptions to stock photo and image websites, such as iStock, allow you to purchase and use high-quality visuals while adhering to licensing requirements.

BOX 8.2. DESIGN RESOURCE HOW TO: COLORIZING AND DOWNLOADING IMAGES WITH ISTOCK

iStock (https://www.istockphoto.com/): iStock is an example of a stock photo and image website. Along with stock photos, iStock offers illustrations. The site offers high-quality stock photos purchased through credits or a subscription. When you purchase a stock photo on iStock, the file comes with a standard license allowing you to modify, resize, and customize an image for your infographic. Because you pay to use the photograph, you do not need to provide attribution. When you purchase and download an image, it will be free of the iStock watermark.

FIGURE 8.2 ■ Refining an Image Search and Entering a HEX Code in iStock

Refine your image search by filtering images.

Enter a Hex code to filter for images that match colors of your infographic.

- Use the "Refine" function to filter your search results for license type, orientation, number of people, and color (Figure 8.2).
- Avoid editorial license photos. They can't be modified and are typically used for real-world events such as news stories.
- To refine pictures by color, enter your HEX code. This will help your stock photo match the color scheme of your infographic (see Figure 8.2).

You will adjust the file size of visuals including photographs, icons, and illustrations for your infographic. Stock photo or image websites will offer a small or medium file size, which is adequate for generating high-resolution images for an infographic (see PLANETS Illustrative Example— Preparing the Mars Photo). Using a large file size for photographs could cause your infographic to load slowly online or make for a large file once you save the infographic. For example, a resolution of 300 dots per inch (dpi) and file size of 72 kilobytes for a photograph will provide a high-quality image in your infographic. For icons, you might find small file sizes under 50 kilobytes will display clearly in an infographic. Remember each image you include in your infographic contributes to the infographic's total file size.

BOX 8.3. PLANETS ILLUSTRATIVE EXAMPLE— PREPARING THE MARS PHOTO

The PLANETS infographic includes a photograph of Mars taken from NASA's Maven mission spacecraft under direction of the Lunar Planetary Institute. Because the photograph is public domain, it is

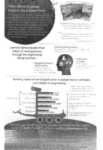

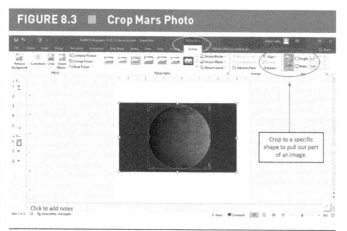

FIGURE 8.3 ■ Crop Mars Photo

NASA/MAVEN/Lunar and Planetary Institute

free for use with a credit citation. We used the Crop function under Picture Tools and Format in PowerPoint to create a circular shape of only the planet. This serves as the background image in the infographic's title (Figure 8.3). We saved the photograph as a JPEG file with a resolution of 300 dpi and file size of 72 kilobytes.

Working With Icons

We recommend selecting simple icons to ease interpretation and maintain harmony across the infographic's visual elements. If you selected icons in Step 4 to represent concepts or data in your infographic, format the icons in Step 8 so they are cohesive and harmonious with your infographic's aesthetic. When searching for icons, you will find many different styles. Common styles include glyph, outline, filled outline, colored shapes, and handwritten icons (Figure 8.4). Some icon styles are more detailed or have heavier line weights than others. Use a consistent icon style with similar line weights or icons within the same family if using multiple icons.

FIGURE 8.4 ■ Different Icon Styles

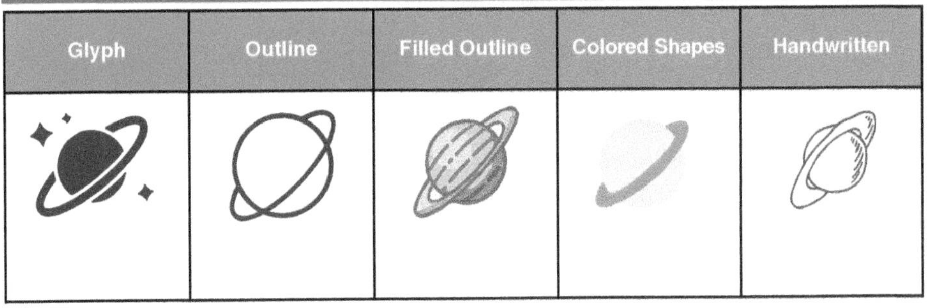

Glyph	Outline	Filled Outline	Colored Shapes	Handwritten

Colorizing and Downloading Icons. If you are incorporating icons in your infographic, you can use websites like Noun Project and Iconfinder to find icons of the same style. Most icon websites offer similar features such as searching for a specific icon, searching within icon families or categories, applying an icon color other than black, and downloading the icon as a raster or vector image type. Some of these websites have expanded to include photos and illustrations. In keeping with your infographic's color palette, with a paid account in Noun Project, for example, you can apply a HEX code before downloading (see Design Resource How To: Colorizing and Downloading Icons With Noun Project). Noun Project also offers an add-in for Microsoft Word and PowerPoint applications, so you can access the icon gallery, colorize, and insert an icon right into your working file. No matter what site you use to select icons, be sure to follow any copyright and attribution requirements.

BOX 8.4. DESIGN RESOURCE HOW TO: COLORIZING AND DOWNLOADING ICONS WITH NOUN PROJECT

Noun Project (https://thenounproject.com/): Like many online resources, Noun Project offers free and paid accounts. With a paid account, you can download icons in custom colors and use icons without providing attribution.

- To download an icon in a custom color, select the color box and insert the HEX code for the color you want (Figure 8.5). We highly recommended applying custom colors to icons in Noun Project before downloading. A free account provides limited options for recoloring your icon. Once downloaded, you can't apply a HEX code to an icon in PowerPoint, and while there are recoloring options, they won't be the exact color.

FIGURE 8.5 ■ Icon Styles, HEX Codes, and File Formats in Noun Project

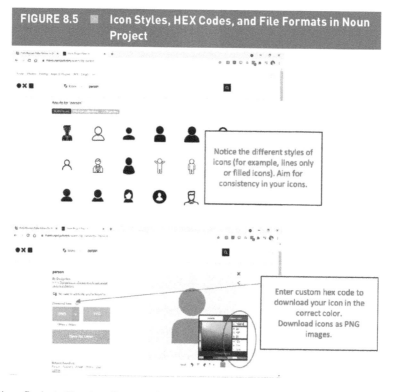

- Noun Project offers two file types for download: PNG and SVG. PNG file types provide a transparent background, so we recommend using this file type in infographics (see Figure 8.5).

Constructing Visuals Using Multiple Icons. A main point or idea might be difficult to capture in one icon. Formatting the color, size, and orientation of multiple icons and layering them into a central image allows you to customize a visual element that represents your message. Layering icons and other visual elements is a fundamental technique you will use throughout the design process in PowerPoint or other platforms. When layering icons in PowerPoint, the "Send Backward" and "Bring Forward" functions designate what visual elements go in front of and behind each other. Use the "group" function to cluster icons and other infographic elements, such as text boxes, as one item. When grouped, you can easily move, align, and distribute multiple visual elements at once. You can ungroup the selection of icons and other visual elements to edit individual items as needed.

In Step 4 of the PLANETS infographic, one of the main points is about "students demonstrating three habits of mind practices shown to enhance student attitudes toward engineering." We selected individual icons for the three "habits"—collaboration, persistence, and success—applied a HEX code to each from our design palette, and downloaded the icons from Noun Project into PowerPoint (see PLANETS Example—Formatting, Layering, and Grouping Icons). For each icon we inserted a text box with a short description of the habit of mind practice and placed them in a list. To visually connect the "mind" concept and the infographic's planetary science theme, we cropped a space photograph to an oval shape, blurred its edges by applying a Picture Effect, and layered it on top of a custom-colored head icon from Noun Project.

Our initial design sketch in Step 7 shows the "habit" icons listed to one side of the head icon, each with its own text box describing the habit of mind. When we constructed it, however, the connection between the "habits" icons and the "mind" icon was weak and the balance was off. To create a stronger visual connection between the icons representing "habits" and the icon representing "mind," we placed the icons inside the head icon by layering them on top of the space photograph and recoloring them white for better contrast. We then grouped all the icons and the space photograph into a single image so they could move together as one visual element. To improve the balance of the text box placement, we encircled the "habits" icons around the head icon. We then grouped the three text boxes and the habits of mind image so that both the text and visual would cluster and move together. As a single object, we could have saved the habits of mind visual as a PNG file and uploaded to an online platform, such as Canva, and inserted into an infographic template as an object.

BOX 8.5. PLANETS EXAMPLE—FORMATTING, LAYERING, AND GROUPING ICONS

The following annotated screenshots demonstrate how to format, layer, and group multiple icons and text boxes to create a visual representation of a main point that is abstract: Habits of mind. We use PowerPoint for the demonstration, and although you may be working from a different version of PowerPoint or different operating platform (i.e., PC or Mac), the basic functions for formatting, layering, and grouping should still be included.

- **Formatting.** We downloaded all icons for the visual using Noun Project, where we applied HEX codes to colorize the icons according to our design palette from Step 5. We inserted the icons, space image, and text boxes into one PowerPoint slide.

We then cropped the image to an oval shape and blurred the edges using a picture effect so that the space image blends nicely with the head icon (Figure 8.6).

FIGURE 8.6 ■ Icon Crop and Blur

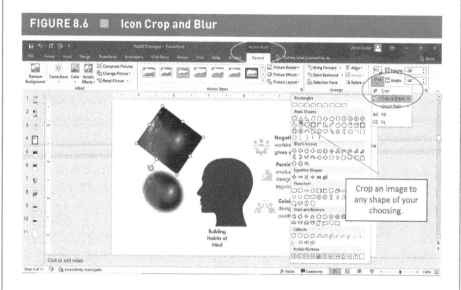

- **Layering.** We used the "Bring Forward" function for the space image and the "Send Backward" function for the icon to layer the space image on top of the head background (Figure 8.7). These functions situated the image and icon relative to each other.

FIGURE 8.7 ■ Icon Layering

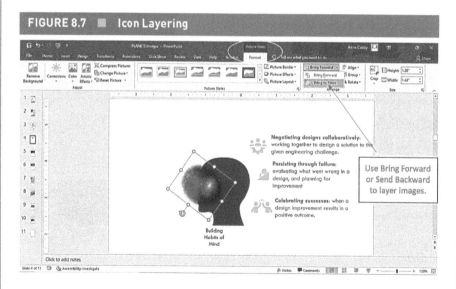

- **Recoloring.** It is best to download icons in the color you need before working in PowerPoint because you will not be able to recolor them to custom colors using HEX codes. However, PowerPoint does offer limited preset options for recoloring

(Figure 8.8). In our case, we needed to recolor an icon to white from our custom color. If you need to change your icon to a different custom color, you will need to return to Noun Project to apply the preferred HEX code and download the icon again.

FIGURE 8.8   Icon Styles, Hex code and File Format in Noun Project

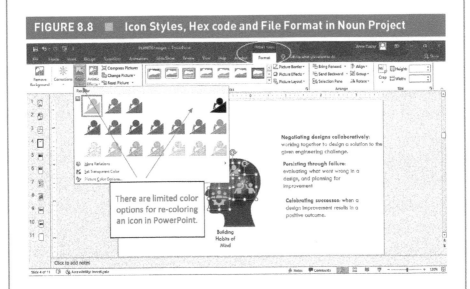

- **Grouping icons.** When you group multiple elements in a visual, you move them as one item, rather than moving each element one at a time (Figure 8.9). After layering our white icons on top of the space image using the "Bring to Front" option, we selected each icon, the space image, and the small text box to group them into one image.

FIGURE 8.9   Icon Grouping

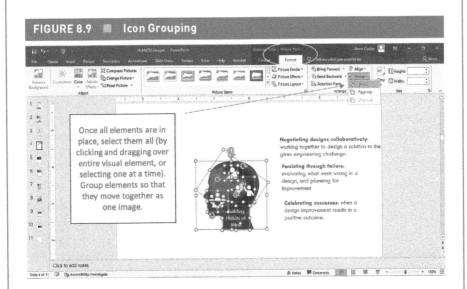

- **Grouping icons and text boxes.** To finalize this visual, we moved the textboxes to orient closely with their corresponding icons and grouped the text boxes and center visual together (Figure 8.10).

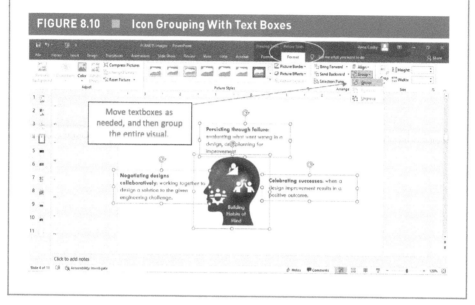

FIGURE 8.10 ■ Icon Grouping With Text Boxes

Working With Shapes

As simple as it sounds, you can create many infographic elements using shapes, icons, and text boxes in PowerPoint. Shapes can form backgrounds, sections and section dividers, and information visuals. Similar to icons, working with shapes requires formatting, layering, and grouping them with other visual elements using the same functions in PowerPoint. You can manipulate shapes in multiple ways including customizing their fill and outline colors, resizing and rotating them, and applying visual effects. Visual effects, such as shadows, reflections, and beveling, can add unnecessary visual clutter and should be used minimally, if at all. Any modifications to shapes should be consistent and harmonious with other visual elements in your infographic.

In Step 4 of developing the PLANETS infographic, we identified a second main point about middle school youth showing statistically significant increases in positive attitudes toward engineering as a result of their participation. The visual for this finding was a bar chart from the evaluation report, but we wanted to make it more visually appealing and connected to the PLANETS project. We decided to replicate the PLANETS mascot, Rosie, which the project uses to represent a Mars rover (PLANETS Illustrative Example—Using Shapes to Construct Visuals). Constructing Rosie involved inserting and editing different shapes and adjusting their color, sizing, and space alignment and distribution. The "Align" function in PowerPoint helps ensure that shapes align with one another and distribute evenly either horizontally or vertically.

This ensures the uniformity of visual displays with repeated shapes or icons. We also used layering and grouping to organize the multiple shapes into one object so we could easily move them within the infographic. We could have also saved the grouped object as a PNG file for uploading into an online template.

BOX 8.6. PLANETS ILLUSTRATIVE EXAMPLE— USING SHAPES TO CONSTRUCT VISUALS

This series of PowerPoint screenshots demonstrates how you can construct a visual image with shapes. Using Rosie the Mars rover from the PLANETS project, the demonstration highlights working with multiple shapes, changing shape color using a HEX code, outlining shapes to give emphasis, aligning and distributing the spacing of shapes, and grouping them to create one image.

- **Multiple shapes.** From the Insert tab, there is an option to select a variety of shapes. We selected rectangles, circles, an inverted trapezoid, and arcs (for the "hands") to construct Rosie. The figure below presents Rosie constructed and deconstructed into her multiple shapes (Figure 8.11).

FIGURE 8.11 ▦ Rosie Multiple Shapes

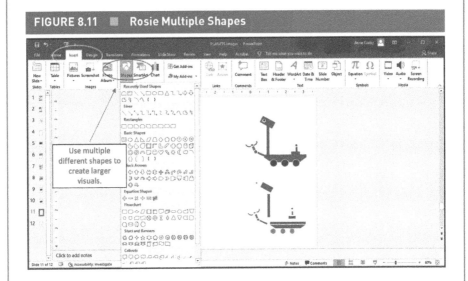

- **Coloring shapes.** When inserting a shape in PowerPoint, there is a default fill color. Change the color of your shapes under the Format tab by entering a HEX or RGB code using the "More Colors" option to specify your preferred color (Figure 8.12).

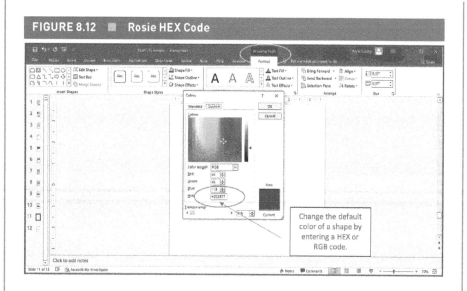

FIGURE 8.12 ■ Rosie HEX Code

Change the default color of a shape by entering a HEX or RGB code.

● **Outlining shapes.** To layer the circular wheels over the base of the rover and accent them some, we added a white outline to the three circles (Figure 8.13). We increased the weight (thickness) of the outline line to make it more visible.

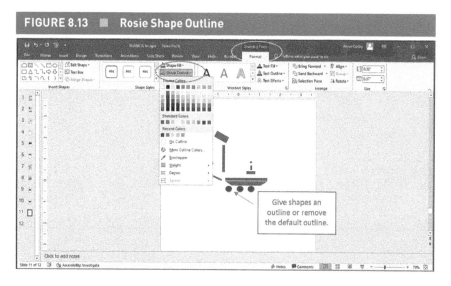

FIGURE 8.13 ■ Rosie Shape Outline

Give shapes an outline or remove the default outline.

● **Aligning and distributing shapes.** Use PowerPoint's "Align" function to align and distribute shapes, images, and icons precisely, rather than moving each one and "eye-balling" if they are aligned and evenly distributed horizontally or vertically (Figure 8.14). "Align Middle" means the middle of the circles are all on the same line, so we used this for the rover's wheels. We also used the "Distribute Horizontally" option to ensure there is equal horizontal distance between Rosie's wheels.

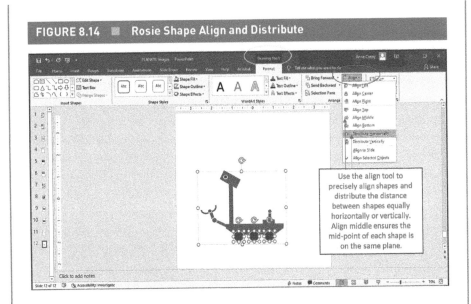

FIGURE 8.14 ▨ Rosie Shape Align and Distribute

Use the align tool to precisely align shapes and distribute the distance between shapes equally horizontally or vertically. Align middle ensures the mid-point of each shape is on the same plane.

- **Grouping shapes.** Once the shapes were in place, we selected them all and grouped them (Figure 8.15). There are multiple ways to select all the objects you want to group, including "Select All" under the Edit tab, dragging your cursor over all the objects to select them, or holding down the Shift key while clicking on each item to group.

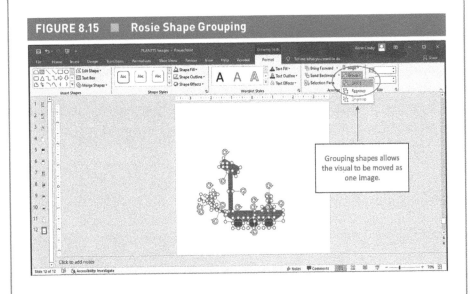

FIGURE 8.15 ▨ Rosie Shape Grouping

Grouping shapes allows the visual to be moved as one image.

Working With Data Visualizations

In addition to fonts, shapes, and text boxes, infographics often contain data visualizations, such as charts and graphs. You might have an existing data visualization from a study report, or you might need to create one for a main point in your infographic. For "how to" instruction on creating data visualizations, we recommend you explore the practical books and workshops from experts such as Stephen Few, Stephanie Evergreen, and Ann Emery. Here, we address how to take a data visualization and format it so it adheres to your infographic design plan through color and font treatments, placement, sizing, and grouping (see PLANETS Illustrative Example—Formatting and Integrating Data Visualizations). As with icons and shapes, once you format a data visualization, you can save it as a PNG file and upload it to an online infographic template, if that is the platform you have chosen.

BOX 8.7. PLANETS ILLUSTRATIVE EXAMPLE— FORMATTING AND INTEGRATING DATA VISUALIZATIONS

This series of screenshots demonstrates how to insert and format a data visualization already created in Excel. It then shows how to integrate it with the Rosie the Mars rover visual to depict a main point in the PLANETS infographic.

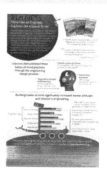

- **Insert Excel bar chart.** To insert the Excel bar chart we had created in the PLANETS report, we copied and pasted it into PowerPoint (Figure 8.16). Because Excel and PowerPoint are both Microsoft Office products, they work fairly seamlessly together. As such, you can still access the Excel data while working in PowerPoint.

FIGURE 8.16 ■ Insert Excel Bar Chart

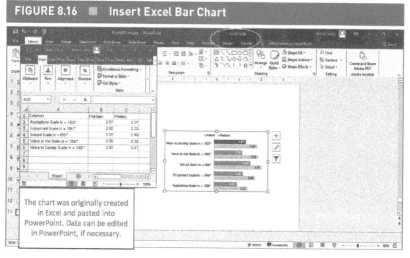

The chart was originally created in Excel and pasted into PowerPoint. Data can be edited in PowerPoint, if necessary.

- **Remove axes.** In this step, we removed any elements of the bar chart that we would not need once integrated with the Rosie visual (Figure 8.17). This included deleting the horizontal and vertical axes and their labels. We added axis labels using text boxes once we inserted the final visual into the full infographic. We retained the data labels that present the mean ratings for each bar in the visualization.

FIGURE 8.17 ■ Remove Excel Axes

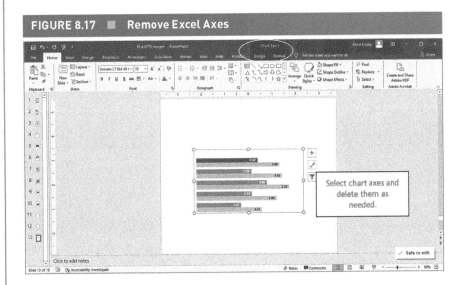

- **Recolor bar chart.** The original bar chart included branding colors from the report, so we needed to change them to the designated colors for the infographic. We selected two colors from our palette that contrasted well and would be appropriate for printing in gray scale. To recolor the bars, we used the format function under "Chart Tools" to enter a fill color using our HEX codes (Figure 8.18).

FIGURE 8.18 ■ Recolor Excel Bars

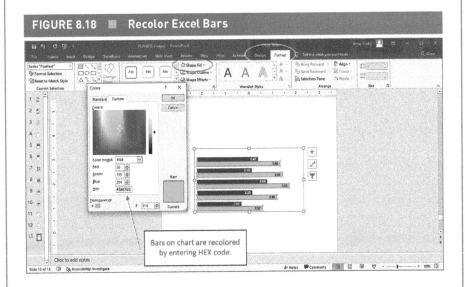

- **Group bar chart and Rosie.** With bar chart formatted appropriately, we placed it next to the Rosie visual. To do this, we used the "Send to Back" function so it was behind the Rosie visual, and we resized it accordingly (Figure 8.19). Lastly, we selected Rosie and the bar chart and grouped them together to become one object.

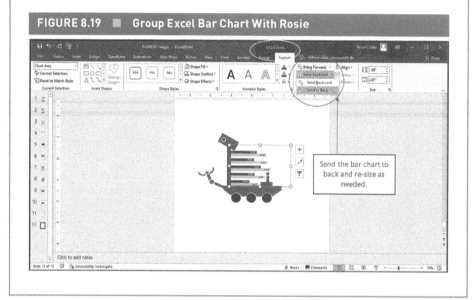

FIGURE 8.19 ▓ Group Excel Bar Chart With Rosie

Up to this point in the construction process you have downloaded, developed, and formatted the visuals for your infographic. When you group all parts that make up a visual into a single object, moving the visual around in your infographic is easier and less time consuming. Grouping eliminates the tediousness of continually readjusting the alignment and distribution of a visual's multiple parts. When grouped as an individual object, you can also right click on it to save it as a picture, which gives you the option to save it as a JPG or PNG file. If you are working in an online infographic template, you can upload the JPG or PNG file into the online platform and add it to your infographic. Remember that a PNG file has a transparent background, which you will need when layering over a colored background in the infographic.

As you develop and format each visual, it is important to revisit your design work in Step 4 to confirm that what you ultimately create still aligns with the story element it represents (e.g., introductory background, main points, and conclusion). Remaining anchored in your design plan ensures that each visual serves a clear and intended purpose for "showing" your infographic's story to your audience. It also results in visual coherence and harmony when formatting is consistent.

BUILDING ESSENTIALS: CREATING THE FOUNDATION

The next step in the construction process involves creating the foundation for your infographic and preparing it for your visuals. The foundation of an infographic includes setting the size of the infographic in your chosen platform and building the layout you selected in Step 5 and drafted in Step 7. During Step 1, you determined how your audience would access and view the infographic, which has implications for sizing your infographic. As described in Step 5, the layout consists of sections, dividing lines, and other visual cues designed with an intentional structure to help the audience navigate your infographic's content. Continuing with the PLANETS infographic, we demonstrate how you can create a foundation in PowerPoint by adjusting the slide size and inserting shapes, divider lines, and images.

Sizing the Infographic

Whether you are working in PowerPoint or with an online infographic template, check the default size of the program and make any adjustments. In PowerPoint, you can enter a custom slide size or select a preset size, such as letter paper, which is ideal if the infographic will be included in a report or printed (see PLANETS Illustrative Example—Sizing the Infographic). If you are creating an infographic poster, enter the poster size requirements. Different infographic template websites use different default sizes. For example, Canva infographic templates are 800 pixels wide by 2000 pixels high, but can be resized with a paid account. Venngage infographics also use a width of 800 pixels, and the height is determined by how much content needs to be included on the infographic. Many of these sites allow for resizing by pixels or inches.

If you are creating an infographic for a particular social media platform, size it accordingly as each has different size requirements typically presented in pixels. For example, if you want to create an infographic for Twitter, the recommended size is 1,200 (h) x 675 (w) pixels, whereas LinkedIn suggests 1,104 x 736 pixels. If you want to tailor your infographic for a particular social media platform, you might need to adjust the design to fit on other platforms. Continually adjusting your infographic design to fit different social media size requirements can be time consuming and could distort your design. An alternative option is to determine the optimal size for your infographic's content, save it as a PDF, and then share it through social media. We discuss dissemination in more detail in Step 10.

If you want to embed your infographic on a website, size it so it is easily readable with different screen sizes. As a general guideline, an infographic that is 1350 (h) x 650 (w) pixels is easily viewable online. It is better for your infographic to be sized too large than too small for digital viewing. However, some infographics are long and require significant scrolling to view fully. Scroll fatigue for infographics is no different than any other form of online media and can disengage your reader.

BOX 8.8. PLANETS ILLUSTRATIVE EXAMPLE— SIZING THE INFOGRAPHIC

We determined in Step 1 that the audience for the PLANETS infographic would primarily view it digitally, but it could also accompany an evaluation report. We originally sized it to fit on letter-sized paper (7.5 x 10.5 inches), but as we brought in all the content, we extended the height to 12 inches (Figure 8.20). This size would still fit on letter-sized paper if printed. To size a slide in PowerPoint, we selected the custom slide size under the Design tab, which allows the user to manually enter specific slide dimensions or preset sizes.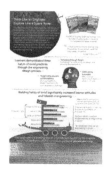

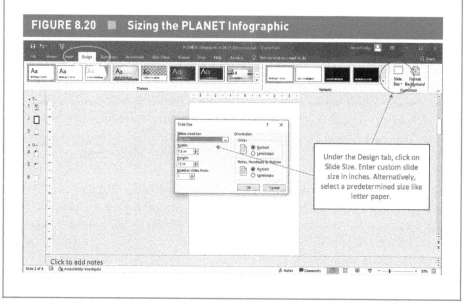

FIGURE 8.20 ■ Sizing the PLANET Infographic

Under the Design tab, click on Slide Size. Enter custom slide size in inches. Alternatively, select a predetermined size like letter paper.

Creating the Background, Sections, and Visual Cues

The first layer of an infographic's foundation sets the background color, if different than white. Create the first layer by inserting a rectangular shape, recoloring it with a HEX code from your design palette, and adding any effects as previously mentioned in this chapter (see PLANETS Illustrative Example—Creating the Background, Sections, and Visual Cues). For example, a slight gradation of color in the background is a subtle effect that can give an infographic a sense of movement and dimension without adding visual clutter. When layering additional elements onto the background, use the "Send to Back" function to anchor the background as the first layer.

If your design plan includes additional boxes or divider lines to demarcate sections, the next step is to insert the appropriate shapes for these. When formatting the size of shapes and lines for the foundation, maintain consistency in size, color, and any effects. Once formatted, place them according to your layout design and set any layering using the "Send Forward" and "Send Backward" functions. Using the "Align" and "Distribute" options ensures you space and align the sections of your layout evenly.

BOX 8.9. PLANETS ILLUSTRATIVE EXAMPLE— CREATING THE BACKGROUND, SECTIONS, AND VISUAL CUES

The foundation of the PLANETS infographic consists of a rectangular shape to set the background color, simple divider lines to demarcate the introduction and main points sections, and a couple of layered photo images to designate the conclusion section.

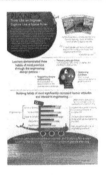

- **Creating the background.** Selecting a long rectangular shape, we created the background of the infographic and applied a lighter gradation of a color from our design palette (Figure 8.21). We also applied a gradient fill under "Format Shape" to add dimension to the background (Figure 8.22).

FIGURE 8.21 ■ **Creating the PLANETS Background**

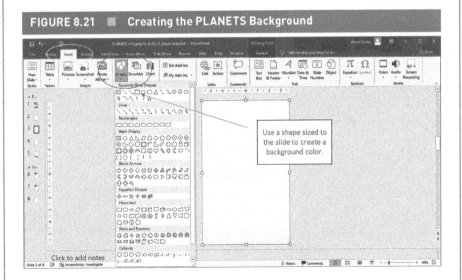

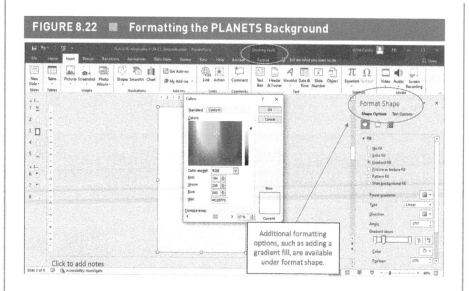

FIGURE 8.22 ■ Formatting the PLANETS Background

- **Creating divider lines.** We used lines to divide the sections of the infographic according to our draft layout in Step 7. We customized the lines under "Format Shape" by adding our custom colors with a HEX code from the design palette with a slight gradation to add dimension (Figure 8.23). Under "Format Shape," you can change the width of a line, create a dashed line, give a line a gradient color fill, and add arrows and other shapes to the beginning or end of a line. These options provide different ways to format divider lines in an infographic.

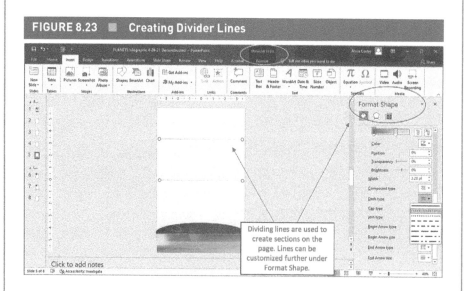

FIGURE 8.23 ■ Creating Divider Lines

- **Layering the background.** We used the "Send Backward" and "Send Forward" function in PowerPoint to organize the layers of what constitutes the infographic's background (Figure 8.24). With these foundational elements in place, we added visuals and text boxes representing the infographic's content.

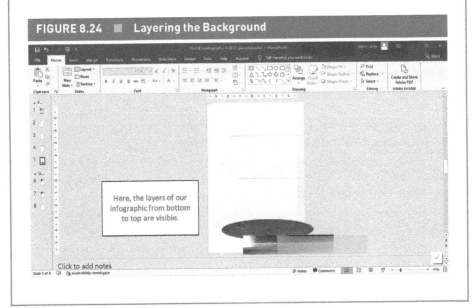

FIGURE 8.24 ■ Layering the Background

BUILDING ESSENTIALS: BRINGING IN VISUALS AND TEXT

With your visuals developed and foundation established, you are ready for the final stage of building your infographic. Although you want to maintain fidelity to the design plan for your infographic, flexibility and adaptability will help bring all the elements together at this stage. For example, sometimes visuals take up more space on the page than envisioned to present well and legibly. By developing your visuals first, you can test if the foundation and layout you designed will accommodate the size and orientation of your visuals. It is easier to adjust the layout around the appropriate sizing of the visuals to promote readability than it is to significantly revise the visuals to fit within a layout.

During this stage, you will also create and bring in any textual information that you didn't create previously as part of a visualization. This could include the title, introductory text, section headers, main point statements, supporting details, a call to action, and credits. In developing textual information, it is easiest to use text boxes, which you can align, distribute, and group with other nearby elements in the infographic. In working with text, refer to the color and font hierarchy you developed in Step 6. This ensures formatting is consistent and harmonious throughout the textual elements of your infographic.

Bringing in visuals and text and layering them onto the infographic's foundation should be a thoughtful process involving careful placement of elements based on your design sketch in Step 7. Two ways to approach this process include building the infographic linearly through the storyline or building around the focal point. Building through the storyline is a beginning-to-end approach that allows the creator to focus on the story as it unfolds. Starting with the focal point is an approach centered on the main visual element designed to grab your audience's attention and interest them in the infographic. A focal point might be a visual element that draws the reader to the beginning of your story, thus rendering these two approaches one in the same.

Determining which of these two approaches or any other approach to take will depend on the number and size of your visuals and the planned layout. For example, if your infographic centers on a single, large visual display, then beginning with your focal point makes sense. If your story includes multiple main points of equal importance, and therefore equal visual emphasis, you might consider building through the storyline.

Regardless of approach, layering in visuals and text onto the foundation of your infographic is a delicate dance between design and purpose. The aim throughout the development process is constructing a visual story that supports the infographic's purpose you articulated in Step 2. The infographic's purpose and the story you developed in Step 3 to achieve that purpose should be the anchor points for design decisions throughout the construction process. Asking yourself the following questions can guide decisions about the placement, size, and inclusion of visuals and text during the construction phase:

- Does this help achieve the purpose of the infographic?

- Does this align with the central message?

- Does this draw attention to or detract from the point I'm trying to make?

- Is the size of this visual appropriate for its purpose in the infographic?

Build Linearly Through the Storyline

The linear approach of building an infographic from the beginning to end of the story engages you as the developer in constructing the infographic as the audience would experience it (see PLANETS Illustrative Example—Build Linearly Through the Storyline). In Step 3, you articulated the story's title, introduction, main points and supporting details, conclusion, and credits. In Step 4, you identified the visuals to represent each of these story elements. With the linear-build process, you layer in the visuals and text of your story by beginning with the title and continuing with each story element through to the credits. Depending on your design sketch, this might mean working from top to bottom of the page as the story unfolds or other story navigation route you designed in your plan.

BOX 8.10. PLANETS ILLUSTRATIVE EXAMPLE— BUILD LINEARLY THROUGH THE STORYLINE

By building the PLANETS infographic linearly through the storyline, we could focus on each visual design element as the story unfolds. This series of screen shots shows how we started at the top of the page with the title and introduction and continued down the page through the story line.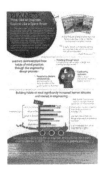

- **Bring visuals into designated sections.** We began at the top of the page with our title and introduction to provide the audience with the project background information necessary to understand the infographic's main points. We brought in the visuals for the title and introduction we identified in Step 4, including our cropped Mars photograph, PLANETS logo, PLANETS curriculum guide image, and a small version of Rosie the Mars rover (Figure 8.25).
We placed the Mars photo in the upper left corner to draw the audience's eye to an entry point to the infographic. Note that the Mars photo is not fully on the page. When we save the file, only items that fall on the page show in the infographic.

FIGURE 8.25 ■ **Bring Visuals Into Designated Sections**

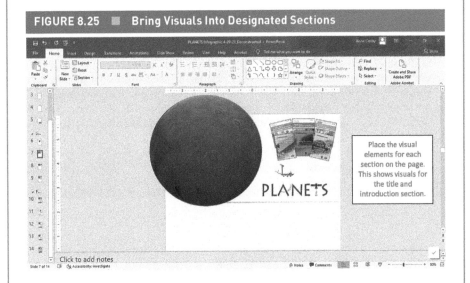

- **Insert and format text boxes.** After moving our visuals into place, we inserted text boxes for the subtitle, introduction, description of the curriculum guides, and a participant quote (Figure 8.26). We adjusted the sizing and placement of visuals for fit and balance on the page. We applied the font treatments from our font hierarchy we developed in Step 6 to each text box. For the introductory text, we layered the text box onto the Mars Photo using the "Send to Front" function. We grouped and aligned all text boxes with their associated visuals. We applied an accent color to the quotation mark icons and grouped them with the participant quote.

FIGURE 8.26 ■ Insert and Format Text Boxes

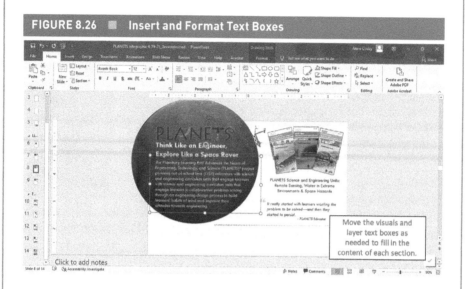

● **Continue to next story element.** Moving onto the next story element, we inserted the habits of mind visual into the following section (Figure 8.27). We formatted its associated text boxes and added an accent bullet using a small star shape that we grouped with each text box. After completing this section for our first main point, we would continue to our second main point in the next section with the Rosie bar chart. We would then continue working down the page to the conclusion and credits sections.

FIGURE 8.27 ■ Continue to Next Story Element

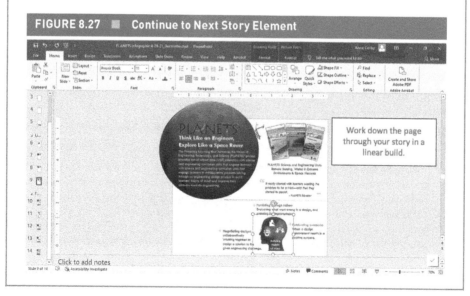

Build Around the Focal Point

With the foundation of an infographic in place, another approach to bringing in visuals is to build around the focal point. Recall from Step 6 of your design plan that a focal point is a visual image that immediately captures the audience's attention when they first glance at the infographic. An engaging focal point draws the audience in and sparks their interest in investing time viewing the rest of the infographic's content. A focal point can be anywhere in an infographic as long as it's strategic and intentional, such as drawing the reader's attention to the entry point (e.g., introduction) or main point of the infographic. As with building an infographic through the storyline, this approach of building around the focal point also requires adjusting the vision of your design plan with what you are able to execute digitally. Still, a carefully crafted design plan serves as your anchor point for design decisions throughout the construction process.

When your design layout from Step 6 calls for a focal point that is center stage to your infographic, then building around your focal point makes sense. Referring to your design layout in Step 5 and infographic sketch in Step 7, begin with placing the focal point as planned and then layer in the other sections, visual cues, and supporting visuals around the focal point. With this approach, be mindful of using visual cues to direct the reader's attention from the focal point to where they should go next in navigating the infographic's story. Keep in mind that people tend to read left to right and top to bottom, so when a focal point resides at the center of the page, for example, the reader needs visual cues showing them what to view or read next. Otherwise, the reader risks wandering through the infographic, missing any important visual or informational connections of the story. Numbering section headers or main points around a focal point is one example of a visual cue that signals to a reader how to navigate the infographic's content around a center-stage visualization. Using white space or different colored section backgrounds are other visual cues that help chunk information and demarcate transition space through the components of the infographic's story.

Another reason to build around the focal point is when you have a focal point as well as other main visuals that could compete for your audience's attention (see PLANETS Illustrative Example—Build Around the Focal Point). With this approach, you begin by adding your focal point and other main visuals to the foundation. Playing with the sizing, coloring, and positioning of your focal point relative to the other main visuals will help you identify where adjustments to your visuals and layout might be necessary. Recall that the size of a visual should represent its relative importance and purpose in the infographic's story. The eyes will also gravitate to saturations of color, therefore starting with your key visuals on the page will help you see what stands out. By beginning with your focal point and main images, you can manipulate them to ensure the focal point remains prominent. Playing with the placement of key visuals relative to each other also helps you implement your plan for balance, flow, and use of white space. Once you size and place these key visuals onto the infographic's foundation, you can add the remaining visual elements and text boxes. During this process, you will want to refrain from adding any extraneous visual elements that clutter the infographic or detract from the infographic's story.

BOX 8.11. PLANETS ILLUSTRATIVE EXAMPLE— BUILD AROUND THE FOCAL POINT

The PLANETS infographic includes the Mars photo image as the focal point as well as two main visuals representing two main points—the habits of mind icon image and the Rosie Mars rover bar chart. We used the Mars image as the focal point to draw the reader's attention to the title and introduction of the infographic. Adding the Mars focal point and two main visuals before other visual elements allowed us to compare the relative emphasis among these three images. We could then determine what adjustments might be necessary to create balance among the three visuals and maintain the Mars image as the focal point. This series of screenshots shows an alternative approach to adding visuals to an infographic's foundation by starting with the focal point and two main visuals and checking for extraneous visuals and clutter that would detract from them.

- **Comparing the focal point and other main visuals.** When we first inserted the Mars image, habits of mind visual, and Rosie bar chart, we could immediately see that Rosie's size was too large relative to the page size and other two visuals (Figure 8.28). At that size she would become the focal point, and there would not be adequate room for the conclusion and credits. We also realized we might need to enlarge the Mars image to maintain its prominence on the page.

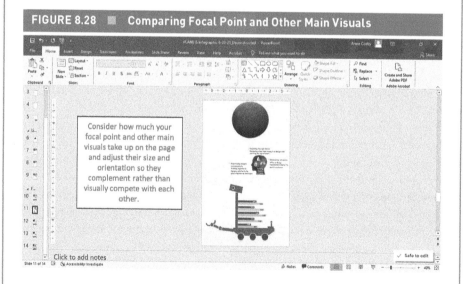

FIGURE 8.28 ▦ Comparing Focal Point and Other Main Visuals

- **Place focal point according to design.** After increasing the Mars image, we placed it according to our design sketch from Step 7 (Figure 8.29). We intentionally did not place the full image on the page to make efficient use of space. We then created our section dividers, brought in the background images for our conclusion and credits sections, and placed the habits of mind and Rosie visuals in their respective sections. We played with the placement of our two main visuals relative to the Mars focal point to determine how best to use white space and create balance on the page.

FIGURE 8.29   Place Focal Point According to Design

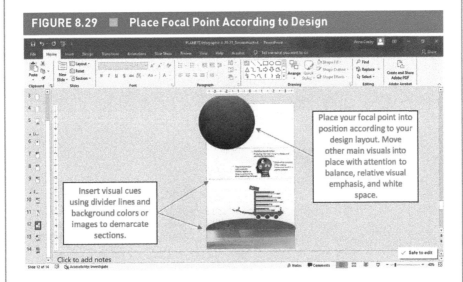

● **Declutter the infographic.** After placing our main visuals relative to the focal point, we brought in the other visual elements. We kept the use of white space in mind and avoided adding extraneous visuals as much as possible. For example, in this screenshot, you can see we considered additional guiding lines between the text boxes and the habits of mind icons, but determined they added visual clutter and removed them (Figure 8.30).

FIGURE 8.30   Declutter the Infographic

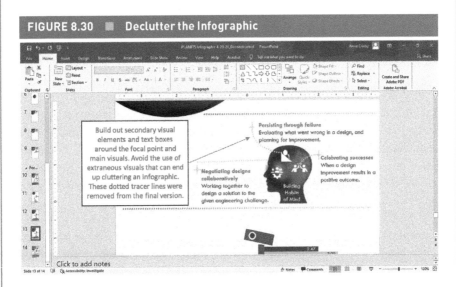

● **Add or remove details for coherence and flow.** With visuals in place, the next step was adding text boxes for our main points, supporting details, source notes, and credits formatted based on the font hierarchy from Step 5. With all visual and text elements in place, we checked for balance, white space, and any details that helped or hindered navigational flow. This screenshot shows how we initially used an arrow to guide the reader from one main point to the next main point, but ultimately decided it didn't add enough visual value to retain it (Figure 8.31).

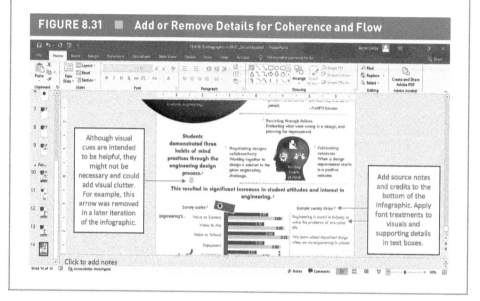

FIGURE 8.31 ■ Add or Remove Details for Coherence and Flow

MAKING YOUR INFOGRAPHIC 508 COMPLIANT

508 compliance addresses accessibility for information and communications technology (ICT) for people with visual, auditory, or other cognitive disabilities. It is a requirement of federal agencies, subcontractors, and grantees to make information accessible to those with disabilities (GSA, 2022), and a best practice in general. Infographics pose unique challenges to 508 compliance because they primarily use visual cues and images to represent information, rather than text, which screen readers translate into speech. Screen readers and other accessibility technologies (e.g., Braille displays and high-contrast modes) may not accurately depict the meaning and purpose of visuals in infographics. Therefore, alternative text for visuals should represent both a description of the visual as well as its context and function within the infographic (Institute for Disability Research, Policy, and Practice, 2021).

When working in PowerPoint, select "Check Accessibility" on the Review tab to identify visuals needing alternative text (Penn State Accessibility, 2018). Use alternative text to describe what is shown visually. A screen reader converts this digital text to spoken words. If you made your infographic using an online template, download a PDF version and insert alternative text using Adobe Pro. The U.S. General Services Administration's Section 508 website offers a variety of resources and training materials for developing accessible products (GSA, 2019).

Color contrast, as discussed in Step 6, also improves accessibility and 508 compliance. Use an online tool, such as WebAim's color contrast checker, to determine if sufficient contract exists between your background and foreground colors. For example, when testing the colors for the PLANETS infographic, there was insufficient contrast between the orangish font color we used for supporting details text and the background color. We consequently had to darken the font color to create greater contrast and improve readability.

BOX 8.12. STEP 8 DESIGN CHALLENGE
DESIGN CHALLENGE: WHAT IF MY VISION AND DESIGN SKETCH ARE MORE COMPLICATED THAN WHAT I CAN BRING TO LIFE?

You might find during the construction process your design ideas don't turn out the way you had envisioned or sketched in Step 7. Maybe the complexity of your design exceeds your graphic ability to create it. Or perhaps space limitations prevent you from incorporating every visual. *What do you do when your design sketch doesn't seem feasible once you try to build it?*

Maintain realistic expectations. When your creative ideas surpass your ability to execute them, stay grounded in why you decided to create an infographic in the first place—to communicate a compelling visual story to your audience. You can achieve the purpose of your infographic through a variety of designs, so choose options commensurate with your graphic design ability, time, and budget.

Simplify your visuals. When your design ideas are too complex, try scaling them back to something simpler. Perhaps this entails creating a more basic version of your original concept. Visuals don't have to be elaborate to convey a compelling message and sometimes a "less is more" approach can be equally, if not more, effective than an overly complex one.

Reduce the number of visuals. If you have more visuals than room on the page, revisit Step 4 in your design plan to identify necessary visuals for communicating your story and eliminate inessential visuals. Consider removing secondary points or supporting details that, while interesting, don't diminish the main points if absent. Your audience might spend 3 to 5 minutes viewing your infographic and will only retain part of what they viewed. By reducing the number of visuals to show your story, you minimize the audience's cognitive load for digesting and recalling the infographic's main points.

Seek help. If you are committed to a creative idea, and time and budget permit, search for online design tutorials or consult with a professional graphic designer. Tutorials and consultants can provide technical guidance on how to create a visual effect, graphic display, or image.

NOW IT'S YOUR TURN!

- Visit an infographic template website (e.g., Canva, Venngage, and Piktochart) and practice the following:
  - Changing the color of a visual element using a HEX code
  - Changing the font typeface and treatment
  - Searching the website's library for an image and inserting it into the infographic
  - Creating a mock data visualization using a chart or graph template from the website's library
  - Uploading an image (e.g., logo, photograph, icon, or data visualization)
  - Downloading the infographic as a PNG file or PDF

- It's time to build your infographic!
  - Download or create the visuals for your infographic and format them according to your design plan. Remember to save photographs as JPEG files and icons as PNG files.
  - Select the platform for your infographic (e.g., PowerPoint or online template) and size it based on where it will live and how your audience will access it.
  - Create the foundational layer of your infographic.
  - Bring in all visual elements and add textual elements.
  - Check for consistent formatting, balance, white space, and flow. Remove clutter.
  - Make the infographic 508 compliant.

RESOURCES

Check it out!

IMAGE AND COLOR APPLICATION RESOURCES

- iStock Photo: https://www.istockphoto.com/

- Unsplash: https://unsplash.com/

- Pixabay: https://pixabay.com/

- Noun Project: https://thenounproject.com/

- Iconfinder: https://www.iconfinder.com/

ONLINE INFOGRAPHIC TEMPLATE SITES

- Canva: https://www.canva.com/templates/?query=Infographics

- Chris Lysy's How to Create an Infographic in Canva: https://freshspectrum.com/how-to-create-a-two-step-infographic-with-excel-and-canva/

- Venngage: https://venngage.com/templates/infographics

- Piktochart: https://piktochart.com/templates/infographics/

PIXEL TO INCHES CONVERTER

- Pixels Converter: https://pixelsconverter.com/pixels-to-inches

508 ACCESSIBILITY RESOURCES

- GSA Section 508's training videos and resources for PowerPoint Accessibility: https://www.section508.gov/create/presentations/

- Training videos on accessible infographics in PowerPoint and Canva: https://www.csun.edu/universal-design-center/accessible-infographics

- WebAim's guidance on alternative text: https://webaim.org/techniques/alttext/

- Fresh Spectrum's blog on Canva and accessibility: https://freshspectrum.com/canva-accessibility/

STEP 9: REVIEW THE INFOGRAPHIC

The review process ensures an infographic accomplishes its purpose with audiences. Your audience might glean exactly what you intend from the infographic if the main points and visuals point to a clear central message. People looking at an infographic with an unclear or obscured central message could misinterpret its meaning. You can learn how people might interpret your infographic by asking a small group to review it before sharing it broadly. Soliciting reviewer feedback on your draft infographic helps ensure your main points and visuals are clear, culturally sensitive, and free of jargon, distractions, and any other sources of confusion or misdirection.

The review process identifies people's interpretations of the infographic's visuals and textual information. The goal of the review process isn't to eliminate multiple interpretations of the infographic as people may have slightly different perspectives on your infographic based on their background and lived experiences. Rather, the review process reveals whether the audience can glean the central message and purpose of the infographic, even through the lens of varied perspectives. It also identifies what visual elements or text might contribute to the audience misinterpreting the infographic's central message and purpose. Reviewer feedback can inform changes to how an infographic presents and visualizes the main points of the story so they better represent and communicate the central message.

In Step 9, you present the infographic you drafted in Step 8 to reviewers for feedback. We recommend saving your draft infographic as a PDF to maintain formatting for review purposes. The type of feedback you request will depend on who you select to review your infographic, and could include in-depth feedback using the Checklist for Reviewing Infographics or less formal, "quick-glance" feedback. We recommend collecting both types of feedback and describe each in this chapter.

CHECKLIST FOR REVIEWING INFOGRAPHICS

The Checklist for Reviewing Infographics presents guidelines for reviewing infographic elements across four components: Story, Content, Design, and Visuals. The checklist includes best practices and can serve as a formative tool for improving the readability, clarity, and quality of infographics. The checklist includes practices described in Steps 1 through 6 of the 10-step infographic development process, so you can use it as a tool in both the design and review process.

Story

As described in Steps 1 through 3 of the development process, the Story element of the Checklist for Reviewing Infographics focuses on the audience (the "who"), purpose (the "why"), and the message (the "what"; Table 9.1). When you view an infographic, you should be able to flow through it easily to discern the story and its central message. Even with complex content, a well-structured story communicated through visual images will help readers understand the central message (Nielsen, 2018; Weinreich et al., 2008). When visuals connect to a storyline in a coherent and easily navigable manner, it not only helps with understanding, but it also enhances the audience's ability to recall meaning (Knaflic, 2015).

As the creator, you should be clear on the audience, purpose, and message for the infographic's story. For reviewers, it might be challenging to identify the audience for an infographic, yet regardless, the purpose and central message should be clear. To the extent reviewers have an understanding of the audience, ask them if the purpose and central message are culturally appropriate for the audience. When an audience is indiscernible or not explicitly named, reviewers might surmise that the audience is broader than a specific group, such as the general public. An infographic could also have multiple audiences, who have slightly different interests in the same story. The audience doesn't need to be explicitly named in an infographic, but reviewers should

TABLE 9.1 ■ Story Element Guidelines From the Checklist for Reviewing Infographics
STORY

The story conveys the main message for the intended audience. It defines the "what," "why," and "who" of the infographic. Audiences flow through an infographic easily with a well-presented story.

AUDIENCE (THE "WHO")

○ The main message and purpose of the infographic reflect the information needs, interests, and background of the intended audience.

PURPOSE (THE "WHY")

○ The infographic conveys why the main message is important for readers by presenting a story with a compelling purpose (e.g., to inform, improve, guide, or catalyze).

MESSAGE (THE "WHAT")

○ The main message is clear and easily identifiable.

be able to infer the audience based the infographic's story and visual elements (see Step 6 for how visual elements can represent specific cultural, social, political, and organizational groups).

When reviewing an infographic based on the guidelines for the Story element, reviewers should discern or correctly infer the intended audience, purpose, and message. For example, in the *Pregnancy and Exercise* infographic from the University of Alberta's Program for Pregnancy and Postpartum Health, the audience, purpose, and message are clear (Figure 9.1). For audience,

---

FIGURE 9.1 ■ Story Element Example: Pregnancy and Exercise

Reproduced from [Infographic. Prenatal Physical Activity: Baby Steps for Better Health, Davenport, M.H., Horbachewsky, T., Brown, M., 54, 360–361, 2020] with permission from BMJ Publishing Group Ltd.

the infographic speaks to pregnant women and possibly health practitioners who provide support and education to women during their pregnancy. This is a clear example of a well-specified audience for an infographic. A reviewer might see the purpose as promoting physical activity throughout pregnancy. The central message is that physical activity is safe and reduces the risk of pregnancy-related illnesses and complications.

Content

The content comprises the substance of an infographic's story and includes the title, introduction, main points and supporting details, conclusion, and credit. The Content element for the Checklist for Reviewing Infographics provides guidelines for each of these story components and includes best practices described in Step 3, Create the Story (Table 9.2). The title should be purposeful, succinct, and interesting (Grant, 2013; Subotic & Mukherjee, 2014). An introduction should include background or contextual information that sets readers up for understanding the main points of the infographic. Reviewers of an infographic should be able to identify the main points, any secondary points (if included), and supporting details of a story and discern how they relate to each other, either hierarchically by level of importance or sequentially, for example. The main points of a story should include visual representation as well as orienting text that supports the audience in gleaning their relevance and meaning (Dunlap & Lowenthal, 2016). Infographics should also include a conclusion or call to action that reinforces the infographic's purpose. The conclusion helps the audience understand why the information you presented matters or what

---

TABLE 9.2 ■ Content Element Guidelines From the Checklist for Reviewing Infographics

CONTENT

The content consists of elements that tell the story. This is the substance of the infographic.

TITLE

○ The title is relevant, engaging, and succinct. It draws the reader in.

INTRODUCTION

○ The introduction lays the foundation for the main message by presenting important background or contextual information.

MAIN POINTS

○ There is an organized hierarchy of information that conveys a memorable message through main points, secondary points, and supporting details.

CONCLUSION

○ Readers know what to consider, what next steps to take, or where to go for more information (e.g., contact information or URL links are included). There is a call to action that reinforces the purpose of the infographic.

CREDIT

○ Sources are credible and cited appropriately.

they might do next. A compelling infographic answers the question "so what?" That is, what do you want the audience to take away or do now that they have viewed its content. Lastly, credits should be included for the relevant information sources of your infographic (Krum, 2014).

When reviewing an infographic for its content, reviewers should be able to identify its story components as listed in the Checklist for Reviewing Infographics. For example, in the ALS Association's *Progress by the Bucketful* infographic, you can see the title plays on the well-known ALS ice bucket challenge used to help raise awareness and funds for ALS (Figure 9.2). The image of the ice bucket beside the title makes this association clear. The zig-zag, light-colored pathway creates a navigational route through the infographic and draws the eye to the upper left entry point. The pathway begins with introductory information about how the ALS fundraising movement began, and it ends with a final box providing more background information with a description of ALS.

In between the beginning and end of the path, you encounter the main point, secondary point, and supporting details for the infographic. As a reviewer, identifying the hierarchy

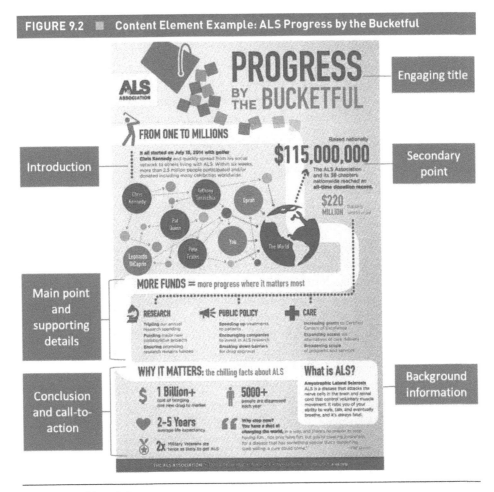

FIGURE 9.2 ■ Content Element Example: ALS Progress by the Bucketful

Source: The ALS Association

among the points of the story exactly as the author intended is not the goal of the review process. Rather it is to distinguish the relative level of importance and visual emphasis of the information included in the infographic as it relates to the overall central message. That is, does the most important information stand out and is its message clear?

We identified the statement "more funds = more progress where it matters most" as the main point of the ALS infographic. However, visually, the eye might be most drawn to the red-saturated world icon with the arrow directing readers to the fundraising amount. In our review, the total fundraising amount is less important than the main point about how ALS funds are used, and that is why we identified the fundraising amount as a secondary point. A different reviewer might perceive these points inversely or equally and argue that the visual emphasis of the secondary point signals its designation as another main point. To bring more visual emphasis to the main point we identified, which may or may not be the main point the author intended, we might suggest slightly decreasing the size of the network visual in the introductory section or revisiting its red color saturations. If a reviewer is unable to clearly discern which of the many points in an infographic are the main points, an author might consider adjusting the size, placement, color treatment, or other design aspects of visuals to give them more emphasis relative to other story components.

Some reviewers might perceive the bottom section of the ALS infographic headed by "Why It Matters" as another main point, but we designated this as the conclusion because it answers "so what" by visually communicating why ALS funds matter. It also includes a call to action, "Why stop now? You have a shot at changing the world…" Through the ALS example, you can see that dissecting an infographic in such a way reveals how the mind processes information, attempts to discern relative importance, and derive meaning. It is also a good example of a visual storyline that creates coherence and connection to the content of an infographic's story.

Design

When executed well, an infographic's design elements—layout, color, font, size, balance, flow, and focal point—coalesce to create a harmonious presentation of the story (Table 9.3). As described in Steps 5 and 6, design elements draw attention to the points of the story by eliminating distractions that clutter or obscure the central message. The layout should organize and structure the contents of the infographic based on the nature of its story (e.g., sequential, categorical, and timeline), keeping in mind a vertical layout supports readers' tendency to read top to bottom of a page (Fessenden, 2018). To help readers flow through an infographic's layout, an infographic should include subtle visual cues such as background shading, section dividers, and section headers that direct the audience's attention from one point to the next. The layout and placement of visuals and text on the page should be balanced and not skewed to one side, top, or bottom of the page. The focal point should connect to the central message and purpose of the infographic and be placed strategically knowing it is what draws readers into the story (Djamasbi et al., 2010). Color and font treatments should be applied consistently and intentionally throughout the infographic with mindfulness for any associations the audience might make with them (Knight & Glaser, 2012; Kulahcioglu & de Melo, 2020; Palmer & Schloss, 2011).

TABLE 9.3 ■ **Design Element Guidelines From the Checklist for Reviewing Infographics**

DESIGN

The design elements work together to create a harmonious presentation of the story. They draw attention to the main message and eliminate distractions that would clutter or dilute the message.

LAYOUT

- o   The type of layout (e.g., timeline, descriptive, categorical, hierarchical/sequential, or comparison) and interactivity (e.g., clickable, animations, video, interactive) is appropriate for the kind of information presented.

COLOR

- o   The color scheme is a simple palette with up to three or four main colors or different saturations of the same color for text and visualizations. Color is used consistently and intentionally to highlight important information. Colors are culturally appropriate and take into account color blindness and black-and-white printing.

FONT

- o   Font size varies based on the hierarchy of information (e.g., larger for headings or main points, smaller for supporting details). Fonts are easy to read, complementary, harmonious, and limited to no more than two or three different typefaces.

SIZE

- o   The size should fit the platform where the audience will view the infographic (e.g., print, social media, website). Vertical orientation can be easier to read than horizontal orientation.

BALANCE

- o   Information is balanced on the page, which directs focus to the main points. The layout is not top or bottom heavy or skewed to one side. White space helps achieve balance among infographic elements.

FLOW

- o   The presentation of images, text, and sections flow with a sense of unity from point to point. There are subtle visual cues that help the reader navigate through the story (e.g., headers, dividers, sections, and color changes).

FOCAL POINT

- o   The design elements draw the reader to a compelling and engaging focal point that supports the main message or directs the reader to an entry point for viewing the infographic.

In revisiting the *Pregnancy and Exercise* infographic, we can see how the design elements support communicating its story and central message (Figure 9.3). The large focal point of the walking pregnant woman immediately captures the audience's attention and directs it to an important statement that supports the infographic's central message that physical activity is safe for pregnant women. Because the focal point illustrates a pregnant woman, it may also increase the intended audience's attention or perception of the information presented as personally

FIGURE 9.3 ▉ Design Element Example: Pregnancy and Exercise

Source: Reproduced from [Infographic. Prenatal Physical Activity: Baby Steps for Better Health, Davenport, M.H., Horbachewsky, T., Brown, M., 54, 360–361, 2020] with permission from BMJ Publishing Group Ltd.

relevant (Zikmund-Fisher et al., 2014). The vertical layout with the title positioned above the focal point makes the infographic's topic clear and sets up a top-to-bottom navigational flow. We would consider the layout to be descriptive. The use of white space and background shading creates balance, demarcates sections, and promotes flow in addition to representing the visual elements of sky and grass. This makes it easy for readers to move from one point to the next. The color palette consists of two complementary primary colors (green and lavender) and an accent color (blue), which are integrated in a balanced manner throughout the infographic. The font appears to be a single typeface with multiple treatments applied consistently according to a font hierarchy. Overall, the design elements come together to communicate a visually appealing, harmonious, and easy-to-navigate infographic.

Visuals

Checklist guidelines for reviewing the visual elements of an infographic focus on their relevance to the central message, interpretability, representativeness, quality, and the extent to which they are the "voice" for the story (Table 9.4). This section of the Checklist for Reviewing Infographics considers icons, data visualizations, photographs, and illustrations as the "visuals" of the infographic. As described in Step 4, an infographic should include visuals that are relevant to the information they represent and be free of extraneous visuals that are not purposeful to the central message. The more visual elements an infographic has, the simpler the data visualizations should be to promote interpretability and readability. Remember that data visualization is part of a larger visual story the infographic is attempting to communicate. Complex data visualizations require time and thought to decipher, and overcrowding an infographic with them can increase

---

TABLE 9.4 ■ Visual Element Guidelines From the Checklist for Reviewing Infographics

VISUALS

Visuals bring life to the story through images, icons, data displays, photographs, and illustrations. Unique visuals that "pack a punch" help readers remember the main message.

RELEVANCE

o Visuals connect to the text and are useful in conveying the main message. They are purposeful, not extraneous.

INTERPRETABILITY

o Visuals are simple, clear, and easy to understand and interpret. They are not cluttered and only include pertinent information and visual elements. The type of visuals (e.g., line graph, bar chart, or icon display) supports interpretability of the data being presented. Visuals are presented truthfully without misrepresentation.

REPRESENTATIVENESS

o The visuals resemble what they are supposed to symbolize. The size of visuals represents their relative importance in telling the story and emphasizes the focal point of the main message.

QUALITY

o Images are high resolution with no blurriness or pixilation. Font and color of visuals are consistent with the rest of the infographic.

VOICE

o The visuals and data "show" the story. The visuals convey a voice that is culturally appropriate for the audience.

the audience's cognitive load, block story flow, and make it more difficult for an audience to connect the elements of an infographic story. To that end, visuals should resemble what you intend them to symbolize and be sized according to their relative level of importance to the points and message of the infographic. To ensure coherence throughout the infographic, visuals should include consistent color and font treatments. One way to test if the visuals serve as the voice for the infographic's story is to focus only on them without reading any text and see if you can glean a main point or message. If you can, the infographic "shows" rather than "tells" the story.

The *Wild Fish Farm Fish* infographic by Jason Petz exemplifies how visuals in an infographic "show" the story (Figure 9.4.) The infographic uses a flow diagram as an anchoring visual element that connects data visualizations, icons, and illustrations in a coherent way that supports readers in navigating through the visual content. The large size of the ocean image with the simple bar chart signals its relative importance to the central message compared to the smaller boxes of icons that represent supporting details. The thickness of the branches in the flow diagram also represents the proportion of the seafood supply coming from various sources (i.e., 64% from wild fisheries, 31% imported, and 5% from extensive fish farming). All visuals

FIGURE 9.4 ■ Visual Element Example: *Wild Fish Farm Fish* Infographic

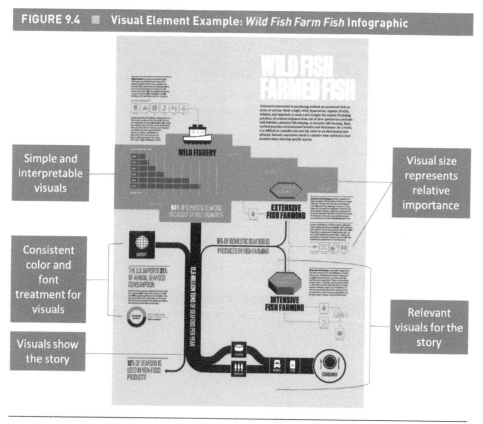

Source: Jason Petz, University of Washington

represent the fishing industry and the story of how farmed fish and wild-caught fish end up on a consumer's dinner plate. All visuals represent a consistently applied color palette.

IN-DEPTH VERSUS QUICK-GLANCE REVIEWS

The Checklist for Reviewing Infographics is one tool for gathering in-depth feedback on an infographic, whereas quick-glance reviews are a less formal way to assess an audience's immediate reaction to what they see. We recommend using both types of reviews to collect a variety of feedback. When following the checklist guidelines, reviewers undergo an in-depth examination of an infographic for the main purpose of providing written, detailed feedback to inform revisions. The guidelines prompt reviewers to consider design elements they might not otherwise notice if looking at an infographic briefly. This level of examination asks reviewers to be consciously aware of things like the intentional and consistent use of color, white space, or navigational prompts that serve as subtle visual cues meant to direct the viewer's attention to an infographic's central message. An in-depth review focuses on how well the design elements help an infographic accomplish its purpose and how it can be improved.

Conversely, a "quick-glance" review gauges if a reviewer can glean an infographic's central message in a matter of minutes. This most closely mimics how an audience will experience an infographic, given people will typically spend an average of five seconds to three minutes viewing an infographic (Krum, 2014; Medina, 2008). The "quick-glance" review assesses immediate and overall impressions and determines if reviewers understand and interpret the infographic's visuals as intended. These reviews are especially helpful when you want feedback on a particular visual or alternate ways of visualizing information. Quick-glance reviews are best conducted in person or through videoconference when you can observe the reviewer reading the infographic and discuss their impressions verbally. This allows you the opportunity to ask targeted questions about their interpretation or reactions to particular visuals or the infographic overall.

SELECTING REVIEWERS

When selecting reviewers, it is important to include individuals who represent a variety of perspectives. Reviewers could include colleagues, the client, the program developer or funder, and individuals representing your intended audience, if different than the aforementioned (see PLANETS Illustrative Example-Review the Infographic). You might also consider including a subject matter expert, a cultural expert, a data visualization expert, or a methodological expert, if appropriate for the nature of your infographic. You might also find reviewers who don't have close knowledge of the topic to make sure the infographic is clear and readable and the central message is evident. Friends and family members are great candidates for quick-glance reviews for this reason. Aim for two to three people to complete the Checklist for Reviewing Infographics and another two to three people to provide quick-glance reviews to ensure you receive constructive and relevant feedback that will guide improvements.

The following are considerations for reviewing the infographic:

- Be sure at least two people provide in-depth feedback using the Checklist for Reviewing Infographics. If you your infographic is data rich, consider including a methodologist or data visualization expert to serve as one of the in-depth reviewers.

- Because they require little effort, put the infographic in front of as many people as possible for a "quick-glance" review. If you have specific aspects you want to test (e.g., did they get the main point, how did they interpret a particular visual, is the language clear, is anything offensive), this is a good way to ask targeted questions and probes for clarification.

- Include representatives of your intended audience in the review process.

BOX 9.1. STEP 9 DESIGN CHALLENGE

DESIGN CHALLENGE: HOW CAN I USE THE REVIEW PROCESS TO DETERMINE IF MY INFOGRAPHIC IS CULTURALLY APPROPRIATE FOR MY INTENDED AUDIENCE?
DESIGN CHALLENGE: WHAT IF I'M UNABLE TO ACCESS OR RECRUIT REPRESENTATIVES OF MY INTENDED AUDIENCE TO REVIEW THE INFOGRAPHIC?

Ideally, you will be able to recruit representatives of your intended audience to participate in the review process, minimally for a quick-glance review. This is especially important if your infographic is intended for members of a particular cultural, social, political, or organizational group, for example. In some instances, you might not know or have access to representatives of a particular group. *How can you ensure the review process captures feedback about the cultural appropriateness of your infographic?*

Focus your review. In addition to the checklist guidelines, you can create an additional set of questions to ask your reviewers. Make the questions specific to your intended audience. Include questions about potential areas of bias or misinterpretation such as choice of color, appropriateness of illustrations and symbols, and interpretation of visuals.

Conduct a "think aloud." Ask reviewers to "think aloud" as they walk through the infographic. Listen to how they interpret what they see. Ask them specific questions about different ways of interpreting a visual. Watch and listen for an affective response to the infographic's visuals or content and ask about their experience without judgment. There is no right or wrong observation during a "think aloud." The purpose is to expand your understanding of how individuals of a particular group interpret, perceive, and experience the infographic differently from you as the creator. This will help you see if what you intended is, in fact, what is accomplished.

BOX 9.2. PLANETS ILLUSTRATIVE EXAMPLE— REVIEW THE INFOGRAPHIC

In Step 8, we drafted the visuals for the PLANETS infographic, created the background and section dividers, and layered in the visuals
and textual elements. When we were creating the draft infographic,
we considered the checklist guidelines. In doing so, we identified
extraneous visual cues, such as directional arrows and connector
lines, that we removed. We tested the color contrast between the
text and background and had to darken the text color to improve
contrast and readability. We also checked the colors for adequate
contrast when printed in black and white. We wanted to include more
white space to improve flow and balance and decrease the appearance of textual clutter. However, the infographic needed to fit on
a single page when printed. This meant the font size for the main
points and supporting details had to be legible and wasn't something

we could reduce to create more white space. Therefore, we had to make a compromise on
the design in order to fit the necessary supporting details.

For Step 9, we sent the PLANETS infographic to the project team, evaluation team, and
colleagues who have expertise in data visualization. We asked the project team and evaluators, who already knew the evaluation results the infographic was presenting, to do a
quick-glance review. This ensured that the visual representation of results with which they
were already familiar was clear and compelling based on their immediate impression. Their
feedback indicated the infographic's central message and main points were clear, visuals
accurately represented evaluation findings, and the color palette was consistent with project branding.

We asked colleagues to complete the Checklist for Reviewing Infographics, and as the
developers, we also used the checklist to conduct a critical review of the PLANETS infographic (Figure 9.5). In examining the infographic against the Story and Content components, reviewer feedback suggested the title, introductory information, main points and
supporting details, conclusion, and sources were clear. They found main points conveyed
the central message articulated in Step 3: "PLANETS activities build learners' habits of
mind and improve their attitudes toward engineering by engaging them in collaborative
problem-solving through an engineering design process." They suggested changes to the
content of the introduction and background information to improve accuracy. Reviewers
also indicated the infographic achieved its purpose as stated in Step 3: "To increase OST
educators' understanding of the learner outcomes resulting from implementation of the
PLANETS curricular units."

When considering the guidelines for the Design and Visuals components, reviewers
noted the vertically oriented layout is appropriately sized to fit on letter paper. Reviewers
agreed the infographic uses a simple color palette with two primary colors (navy blue and
dark sienna) and an accent color (turquoise) and applies these colors consistently to text
and visuals. The infographic uses a single font type with multiple treatments to represent
the hierarchy established in Step 6. Sections of the infographic are demarcated with dotted
divider lines between main points and images and shading for the conclusion and sources

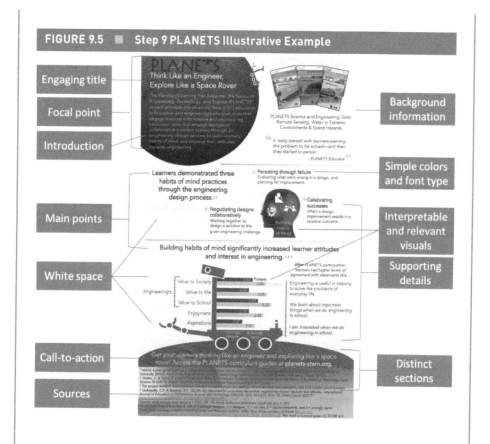

FIGURE 9.5   Step 9 PLANETS Illustrative Example

sections. Although the visuals for the main points drew reviewers' immediate attention, the size and placement of the Mars image in the upper left corner was the focal point that signaled where to begin reading the infographic. Reviewers found the visuals to be appealing and interpretable with the supporting textual details around the habits of mind and rover visuals. They thought the positioning of the visuals was balanced on the page and promoted logical flow for navigating the infographic.

NOW IT'S YOUR TURN!

- Find an infographic online at Cool Infographics (https://coolinfographics.com/) and apply the Checklist for Reviewing Infographics.
  ○ Could you discern the audience, purpose, and central message? If so, what about the infographic made those elements clear?
  ○ Were the story elements easy to identify? If not, why not? What might the developer have done differently to present and visualize any main points?

     ○   Based on the guidelines, what feedback would you offer to improve the design and visuals?

- Send your infographic out for review. Identify peers, clients or funders, representatives of your intended audience, and even friends and family members who might be willing to review your infographic. Select two reviewers to use the Checklist for Reviewing Infographics and ask two others to engage in a quick-glance review.

RESOURCES

Check it out!

- Visme blog on infographic best practices: https://visme.co/blog/infographic-best-practices/
- Stephanie Evergreen's data visualization checklist: https://stephanieevergreen.com/wp-content/uploads/2019/06/EvergreenDataWorkshopPacket.pdf

STEP 10: REVISE, FINALIZE, AND SHARE

LEARNING OBJECTIVES

In Step 10, you will learn how to

- revise an infographic while staying true to your design plan,

- facilitate the editing and finalization process, and

- prepare and share your infographic with your intended audience.

With reviewer feedback from Step 9, in Step 10 you will revise, edit, and finalize your infographic. Integrating reviewer feedback into infographic revisions and having your infographic carefully edited help ensure your infographic is typo free, accurate, visually appealing, interpretable, and culturally sensitive. Investing time in revising your infographic based on reviewer feedback improves the likelihood your infographic will accomplish its intended purpose. The revision and finalization process is not one to short shrift.

REVISING AN INFOGRAPHIC

Reviews based on the Checklist for Reviewing Infographics and quick-glance feedback provide relevant and detailed information about how the audience may interpret and understand your infographic. If you were diligent in planning Steps 1 through 3 and engaged a client, funder, or audience representative early in the process, you should not have to revisit these steps. The foundation of the story—background information, main points and supporting details, and conclusion—should be cohesive. You might need to elevate the visibility of the main points of the infographic or revise content for clarity or accuracy.

Feedback might call for revisiting choices you made in Steps 4 through 6 about visuals, layout, and design to better communicate the infographic's story. This could include identifying new visuals, such as icons that are more culturally appropriate or representative. You might need to adjust the layout and visual cues to improve how a reader navigates through the infographic. You might revise your color and font hierarchy or improve the consistency of its application.

As you collate feedback, themes may emerge as reviewers notice the same things or make similar interpretations. Feedback substantiated in multiple instances either affirms an aspect of the infographic (what is working) or signals a necessary revision (what is not working). You might also receive feedback that is only substantiated in a single instance, but it is on target with the guidelines and worth implementing. Take time to consider all feedback with the understanding that some suggestions might not be relevant to the infographic's message, in keeping with best design practices, or culturally sensitive. For example, if a reviewer suggests a color not included in a brand's palette or one the intended audience might find offensive, you would not make the change.

If revisions are extensive, consider sending the infographic to a subset of prior reviewers for another round of review; in particular, include those who offered the most substantial and relevant feedback. You want to ensure that any substantive revisions meet checklist guidelines and communicate what you intend to convey. Continue iterating until the infographic responds to reviewer feedback and meets the checklist guidelines to the extent practicable, given any constraints or limitations, such as page length, time and budget, and design ability.

EDITING AND FINALIZING AN INFOGRAPHIC

Once you complete revisions based on reviewer feedback, the infographic is almost ready for editing and finalizing (see PLANETS Illustrative Example—Revise and Finalize the Infographic). Before editing, update any alternative text for your visuals and run another accessibility check on your infographic to ensure it is accessible for individuals with disabilities (see Step 8). Also determine if you want to add a copyright or Creative Commons license to your infographic, if you haven't already (see Steps 3 and 4). Lastly, if your infographic will have an online landing page, be sure to include the URL address as a clickable link so the original infographic is always accessible regardless how it's shared (Krum, 2014).

If a professional editor is not within your budget, ask a peer or colleague to help. Request the editor check for general copyedits (grammar, spelling, punctuation), consistent use of formatting (e.g., font size variations, color variations, icon type), data reporting accuracy (e.g., correct labeling and presentation of statistical information), and image quality. Because infographics generally should use as little text as possible, the editor should also look to eliminate unnecessary text without losing meaning. Also make sure the editor verifies all sources and any URLs or hyperlinks. You will make any further revisions to the infographic based on the editor's feedback to finalize the infographic.

BOX 10.1. PLANETS ILLUSTRATIVE EXAMPLE— REVISE AND FINALIZE THE INFOGRAPHIC

In Step 9, we collected helpful feedback from reviewers through the Checklist for Reviewing Infographics and quick-glance reviews. Reviewer feedback primarily focused on textual information in the introduction and background sections. We considered all reviewer feedback, asked follow-up questions to ensure we understood the feedback correctly, and made revisions. For example, we revised the description under the visual of the PLANETS curriculum guides in the upper-right-hand corner to more accurately represent the organization and names of the materials. We changed terminology based on reviewer feedback to more accurately represent the PLANETS program. We incorporated most, but not all feedback. For example, one reviewer thought the small rover by the title was unnecessary, but we decided to retain it to help readers make a visual association between the term "rover" and the image we used to represent it. It might seem extraneous, but we didn't want to assume the audience would know what a Mars rover looks like. We also thought it added an element of fun and might make readers more curious to learn more.

We also had a discussion with members of the project evaluation team about the title. An earlier version of the title was "Think Like a Scientist. Act Like a Space Rover." The first part of the title was intended to tie to the habit of mind component of the PLANETS program. However, reviewers pointed out that the program focuses on thinking like an engineer, so we revised it to "Think Like an Engineer." The think/act format was a play on the "think globally, act locally" slogan and intended to capture the audience's attention. Because Mars rovers explore and collect data, we thought this paralleled what students do in the PLANETS program. However, reviewers thought "explore" was a more accurate term than "act" to represent how students use data, so we made that revision. Following these revisions, we had the infographic professionally edited. Once revised and edited, we shared the infographic with the project team for final approval and use for project reporting and dissemination to OST educators.

The following are considerations for revising and finalizing an infographic:

- Make sure revisions remain aligned with the infographic's purpose and central message and culturally appropriate for the intended audience.

- If reviewer feedback calls for substantive revisions, such as revisiting the purpose and central message of an infographic or replacing a main visual, send the revised infographic back out for review.

- Have the infographic thoroughly edited before finalizing.

SHARING AN INFOGRAPHIC

Once finalized, save your infographic as an image file (JPEG or PNG) or a portable document format (PDF) for sharing (see PLANETS Illustrative Example—Format the Infographic). These file types should be available across design platforms including PowerPoint, online templates, and sophisticated design programs. If the infographic will live online, saving it as a JPEG results in a smaller image file. The smaller image file makes online viewing and sharing easy. However, the compressed size can reduce image quality and make it unsuitable for printing. Saving a PNG file does not reduce image quality, which means the infographic can be resized larger or smaller and retain its quality. As covered in Step 8, a PNG file also has a transparent background, which is ideal when placing an image on a colored background. This may or may not be relevant for your infographic. The disadvantage of a PNG file is the larger file size, which makes it less ideal compared to JPEGs for online viewing. If you know the infographic will be printed, PDF is the preferred format because the file is identical to your original infographic; that is, a PDF does not compress an image like JPEG and PNG files. PDF files are also appropriate if an infographic includes interactive elements such as hyperlinks and popups. PDF files are not easily embedded online, such as in blogs, so if you want to promote online sharing, use a JPEG or PNG file format instead.

BOX 10.2. PLANETS ILLUSTRATIVE EXAMPLE— FORMAT THE INFOGRAPHIC

To save the PLANETS infographic as an image in PowerPoint, we followed these steps (Figures 10.1 and 10.2):

- From the Edit menu we chose "Select All" to capture all the elements on the page.
- We then used the "Group" feature on the Format Shape tab to group all the elements together as a single object.
- Nex, we clicked on the infographic, to view the single box. This is how we knew all elements were grouped into one object.
- We right clicked on the box, and from the popup menu selected "Save as Picture." We then had the option to save it as a JPEG or PNG file.

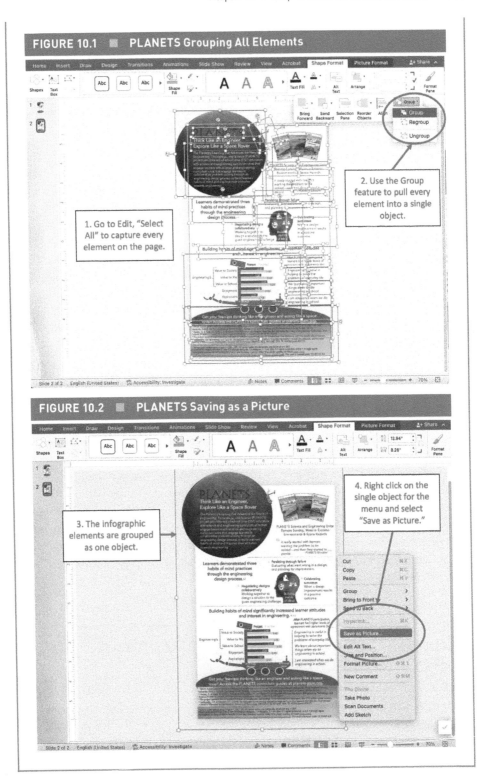

FIGURE 10.1   PLANETS Grouping All Elements

1. Go to Edit, "Select All" to capture every element on the page.

2. Use the Group feature to pull every element into a single object.

FIGURE 10.2   PLANETS Saving as a Picture

3. The infographic elements are grouped as one object.

4. Right click on the single object for the menu and select "Save as Picture."

How you share an infographic depends on how you planned for the intended audience to access it in Step 1. Your audience may be a specific group of people or broadly intended for wider audiences, and your dissemination strategy should reflect as much. You might share an infographic in a document, such as a client report, post on social media, feature in a blog post, or include on a website. You might plan a coordinated approach using multiple platforms to reach your audience (Smiciklas, 2012). If that is the case, you need to determine where the original infographic will live before it is shared through multiple outlets.

Creating a Landing Page

Typically, an infographic intended for broader sharing will have a landing page on a website. This could be your website or a client's website, for example. The infographic can reside on a webpage as an image and the URL included in social media posts, emails, e-newsletters, or other dissemination outlets. Using features such as embed code or share buttons can also help your audience share the infographic from a website. An embed code is HTML code that you can display on the website underneath the infographic. Anyone interested in including the infographic in a blog or publication can copy the code and paste it in their online publication. When someone views their publication, the infographic image will display from your website, not theirs. You can also include credits for the infographic in the code. There are websites that provide embed code generators, and *Infographic Journal* offers an embed code plugin for WordPress. Share buttons are icons that link to different social media platforms that allow viewers to easily share the infographic through social media. Online services, such as ShareThis, will generate a block of share buttons with HTML code for your landing page.

Posting to Social Media

If your infographic will live on a particular social media platform your audience accesses, such as a Facebook group, then you should have sized your infographic accordingly when you drafted the infographic in Step 8. If your infographic lives on a website, but you want to promote it through social media or a blog, you would post it as an image with the URL so that when clicked, it takes viewers to the original document on the website. When promoting through social media, be sure to use multiple channels and ask colleagues, clients, and any other appropriate networks to also share the post. If you created the infographic using an online platform, such as Canva, look for a feature to share it directly to the social media platform of your choosing (see Design Resource: Sharing the Infographic Using Canva).

BOX 10.3. DESIGN RESOURCE—SHARE THE INFOGRAPHIC USING CANVA

Canva, as well as other online platforms that offer infographic templates, offer multiple ways to share an infographic. You can download an infographic as a PDF, PNG, or JPEG file. You can share it directly to multiple social media platforms. For example, you can pull an infographic into a Canva presentation, get a QR code to share, and generate embed code to include on a website (Figure 10.3)

FIGURE 10.3 ■ Sharing the Infographic Using Canva

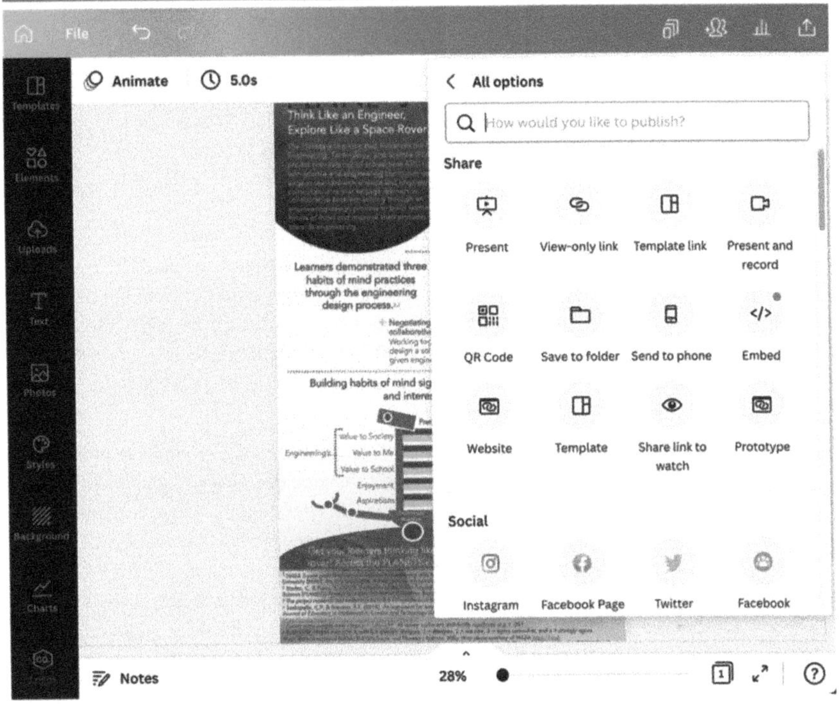

Embedding in a Report

In Step 5, you considered options for the infographic's layout based on how your audience would access the infographic. If the infographic exists within a report or text document, especially one that might be printed, saving it as a PDF and merging it with the final report in PDF would retain the image quality of the infographic. You can also insert the infographic as a JPEG image directly into your word processing file, just keep in mind the image might not appear on the page identically to the original.

The following are considerations for sharing an infographic:

- Save the infographic in the appropriate file format for how you will disseminate it (e.g., JPEG, PNG, or PDF).

- Create a landing page for the infographic so the audience will view the infographic from the landing page, regardless of how it is shared.

- Include share buttons and embed code on the landing page to encourage further dissemination of the infographic.

- Post the infographic to social media with an image of the infographic and link that takes the audience to the landing page to view the infographic.

BOX 10.4. STEP 10 DESIGN CHALLENGE

DESIGN CHALLENGE: WHAT IF REVIEWER FEEDBACK IS CONTRADICTORY OR UNFEASIBLE TO EXECUTE?

If several reviewers provide feedback on your infographic, it is possible you will receive suggestions that conflict with each other or that are beyond the scope of what you can feasibly develop or implement. Perhaps reviewers interpret the same visual in opposing ways. This is valuable feedback as it represents the various interpretations your broader audience might make. You might also grapple with a recommendation that exceeds your design ability or falls outside the purpose and message of the story. *When reviewer feedback is contradictory or unfeasible to implement, what can you do?*

Probe for clarity. Before you make any changes, ask reviewers why they reacted to or interpreted a visual they way they did. Seek to understand their thinking behind a suggestion, particularly if it conflicts with other feedback. For example, one reviewer might dislike a photograph because they think it doesn't represent a cultural group accurately, whereas another reviewer might love the photograph because the colors are harmonious with the rest of the infographic. Understanding the reasons behind conflicting suggestions (e.g., keep or change the photograph) will inform the revisions you make to resolve contradictory feedback.

Try alternatives. If two people interpret the same visual in contrasting ways, try creating a couple alternatives and seek additional feedback to see if you can reach consensus. For example, reviewers might perceive the symbolism or meaning of an icon very differently, in which case, you would seek alternative icons, present them to reviewers, and determine which one reviewers interpret similarly.

Stay aligned with best practices. Sometimes reviewer feedback represents a personal aesthetic or style preference, so when it conflicts with feedback from other reviewers, let the guidelines be your judge. Determine which feedback most closely aligns to the Checklist for Reviewing Infographics as well as the research you might have conducted on your audience's cultural, social, political, or organizational background. It is also important to recognize that every aspect of an infographic may not please everyone, and that is okay.

Know and communicate the limits. Sometimes reviewers suggest substantive changes that are beyond what you can accomplish within your timeframe, budget, or design capability. If this occurs, consider reengaging reviewers in a discussion about the scope and purpose of the infographic to help them understand the limitations with which you are working. With more context, they might adjust their feedback to be more feasible. It is highly likely reviewers won't understand the time, budget, or design implications of their suggestions, so communicating limitations is important in arriving at practicable solutions.

NOW IT'S YOUR TURN!

- Search online for infographics and notice the different platforms for dissemination.
  - How are infographics posted on social media platforms? Is there a thumbnail image that links to a PDF? Is the post itself an infographic, such as the ones you can create using an online template appropriately sized for specific social media platforms?
  - What do you observe about infographics embedded on websites? Is there a thumbnail image that links to a PDF or is it embedded as an image that is fully displayed on a webpage?

- Revise, finalize, and share your infographic! You are now ready to delve into the iterative revisions process, editing, and sharing. If a professional editor isn't in your budget, look to a colleague or peer to provide a copyedit for typos and grammatical mistakes. Once you finalize the infographic, save it as a PDF or image, and share it with your audience. Congratulations! You did it!

RESOURCES

Check it out!

- **Seven tips for displaying an infographic on a website:** https://www.infographicdesignteam.com/blog/wondering-how-to-display-infographics-on-your-website-effectively-7-sure-fire-tips-to-try-out/

- **Use Pixlr to resize photos**: https://pixlr.com/

- *Infographic Journal's* **embed code generator:** https://infographicjournal.com/embed-code-generator/

- **ShareThis** free image share buttons to expand the audience for your infographic on social networks: https://sharethis.com/platform/

CHECKLIST FOR REVIEWING INFOGRAPHICS

This checklist presents guidelines for reviewing infographic elements across four components: story, content, design, and visuals. It reflects best practices in the field of infographics and is intended to serve as a formative tool in improving the quality and utility of infographics. The checklist complements our *10 Steps to Creating an Infographic,* so you can use it as a tool in both the design and review processes.

STORY

The story conveys the main message for the intended audience. It defines the "what," "why," and "who" of the infographic. Audiences flow through an infographic easily with a well-presented story.

○ **AUDIENCE (THE "WHO")**

The main message and purpose of the infographic reflect the information needs, interests, and background of the intended audience.

○ **PURPOSE (THE "WHY")**

The infographic conveys why the main message is important for readers by presenting a story with a compelling purpose (e.g., to inform, improve, guide, or catalyze).

○ **MESSAGE (THE "WHAT")**

The main message is clear and easily identifiable.

FEEDBACK FOR IMPROVING THE STORY

CONTENT

The content consists of elements that tell the story. This is the substance of the infographic.

○ **TITLE**

The title is relevant, engaging, and succinct. It draws the reader in.

○ **INTRODUCTION**

The introduction lays the foundation for the main message by presenting important background or contextual information.

○ **MAIN POINTS**

There is an organized hierarchy of information that conveys a memorable message through main points, secondary points, and supporting details.

○ **CONCLUSION**

Readers know what to consider, what next steps to take, or where to go for more information (e.g., contact information or URL links are included). There is a call to action that reinforces the purpose of the infographic.

○ **CREDIT**

Sources are credible and cited appropriately.

FEEDBACK FOR IMPROVING THE CONTENT

DESIGN

The design elements work together to create a harmonious presentation of the story. They draw attention to the main message and eliminate distractions that would clutter or dilute the message.

LAYOUT

○ The type of layout (e.g., timeline, descriptive, categorical, hierarchical/sequential, or comparison) and interactivity (e.g., clickable, animations, video, interactive) is appropriate for the kind of information presented.

COLOR

○ The color scheme is a simple palette with up to three or four main colors or different saturations of the same color for text and visualizations. Color is used consistently and intentionally to highlight important information. Colors are culturally appropriate and take into account color blindness and black-and-white printing.

FONT

○ Font size varies based on the hierarchy of information (e.g., larger for headings or main points, smaller for supporting details). Fonts are easy to read, complementary, harmonious, and limited to no more than two or three different typefaces.

SIZE

○ The size should fit the platform where the audience will view the infographic (e.g., print, social media, website). Vertical orientation can be easier to read than horizontal orientation.

BALANCE

○ Information is balanced on the page, which directs focus to the main points. The layout is not top or bottom heavy or skewed to one side. White space helps achieve balance among infographic elements.

FLOW

○ The presentation of images, text, and sections flow with a sense of unity from point to point. There are subtle visual cues that help the reader navigate through the story (e.g., headers, dividers, sections, and color changes).

FOCAL POINT

○ The design elements draw the reader to a compelling and engaging focal point that supports the main message or directs the reader to an entry point for viewing the infographic.

FEEDBACK FOR IMPROVING THE DESIGN

VISUALS

Visuals bring life to the story through images, icons, data displays, photographs, and illustrations. Unique visuals that "pack a punch" help readers remember the main message.

RELEVANCE

○ Visuals connect to the text and are useful in conveying the main message. They are purposeful, not extraneous.

INTERPRETABILITY

○ Visuals are simple, clear, and easy to understand and interpret. They are not cluttered and only include pertinent information and visual elements. The type of visuals (e.g., line graph, bar chart, or icon display) supports interpretability of the data being presented. Visuals are presented truthfully without misrepresentation.

REPRESENTATIVENESS

○ The visuals resemble what they are supposed to symbolize. The size of visuals represents their relative importance in telling the story and emphasizes the focal point of the main message.

QUALITY

○ Images are high resolution with no blurriness or pixelation. Font and color of visuals are consistent with the rest of the infographic.

VOICE

○ The visuals and data "show" the story. The visuals convey a voice that is culturally appropriate for the audience.

OBSERVATIONS ABOUT THE VISUALS

REFERENCES

INTRODUCTION

Babb, J. (2003, August). *Mathematical concepts and proofs from Nicole Oresme: Using the history of calculus to teach Mathematics.* Paper presented at the 7th International History, Philosophy and Science Teaching Conference. https://core.ac.uk/download/pdf/144470649.pdf

Balkac, M., & Ergun, E. (2018). Role of infographics in healthcare. *Chinese Medical Journal, 131*(20), 2514.

Beegel, J. (2014). *Infographics for dummies.* John Wiley & Sons.

Bobek, E., & Tversky, B. (2016). Creating visual explanations improves learning. *Cognitive Research: Principles and Implications, 1*(1), 1–14.

Cairo, A. (2016). *The truthful art: Data, charts, and maps for communication.* New Riders.

Clark, R. C., & Mayer, R. E. (2016). *E-learning and the science of instruction: Proven guidelines for consumers and designers of multimedia learning.* John Wiley & Sons.

Dick, M. (2013). Interactive infographics and news values. *Digital Journalism.* https://doi.org/10.1080/21670811.2013.841368

Dick, M. (2015). Just fancy that: An analysis of infographic propaganda in The Daily Express, 1956 - 1959. *Journalism Studies, 16*(2), 152–174.

Djamasbi, S., Siegel, M., & Tullis, T. (2010). Generation Y, web design, and eye tracking. *International Journal of Human-Computer Studies, 68*(5), 307–323.

Dunlap, J. C., & Lowenthal, P. R. (2016). Getting graphic about infographics: Design lessons learned from popular infographics. *Journal of Visual Literacy, 35*(1), 42–59.

Featherstone, R. M. (2014). Visual research data: An infographics primer. *Journal of the Canadian Health Libraries Association, 35*(3), 147–150.

Kemp, M. (2007). *Leonardo da Vinci.* Oxford University Press.

Koch, T. (2005). *Cartographies of disease: Maps, mapping, and medicine.* ESRI Press.

Krum, R. (2014). *Cool infographics: Effective communication with data visualization and design.* John Wiley & Sons.

Lankow, J., Ritchie, J., & Crooks, R. (2012). *Infographics: The power of visual storytelling.* John Wiley & Sons.

McCrorie, A. D., Donnelly, C., & McGlade, K. J. (2016). Infographics: Healthcare Communication for the digital age. *The Ulster Medical Journal, 85*(2), 71–75.

Medina, J. (2008). *Brain rules: 12 principles for surviving and thriving at work, home, and school.* Pear Press.

Nadj, M., Maedche, A., & Schieder, C. (2020). The effect of interactive analytical dashboard features on situation awareness and task performance. *Decision Support Systems, 135*, 113322. https://doi.org/10.1016/j.dss.2020.113322

Nelson, D. L., Reed, V. S., & McEvoy, C. L. (1977). Learning to order pictures and words: A model of sensory and semantic encoding. *Journal of Experimental Psychology: Human Learning and Memory, 3*(5), 485.

Nielsen, J. (2018). *How little do users read? Nielsen Norman Group.* Retrieved January 10, 2021, from https://www.nngroup.com/articles/how-little-do-users-read/

Otten, J. J., Cheng, K., & Drewnowski, A. (2015). Infographics and public policy: Using data visualization to convey complex information. *Health Affairs, 34*(11), 1901–1907.

Paivio, A. (1971). Imagery and language. In S. Segal (Ed.),

Imagery (pp. 7–32). Academic Press.

Smiciklas, M. (2012). *The power of infographics: Using pictures to communicate and connect with your audiences.* Que Publishing.

Tufte, E. R. (1983). *The visual display of quantitative information.* Graphics Press.

Tufte, E. R. (1997). *Visual explanations: Images and quantities, evidence and narrative.* Graphics Press.

Utt, S. H., & Pasternack, S. (1993). Infographics today: Using qualitative devices to display quantitative information. *Newspaper Research Journal, 14*(3, 4), 146–158.

Weinreich, H., Obendorf, H., Herder, E., & Mayer, M. (2008). Not quite the average: An empirical study of Web use. *ACM Transactions on the Web (TWEB), 2*(1), 1–31.

Zopf, R., Giabbiconi, C. M., Gruber, T., & Müller, M. M. (2004). Attentional modulation of the human somatosensory evoked potential in a trial-by-trial spatial cueing and sustained spatial attention task measured with high density 128 channels EEG. *Cognitive Brain Research, 20*(3), 491–509.

Zull, J. E. (2002). *The art of changing the brain.* Stylus.

CHAPTER 1

Duarte, N. (2008). *Slide:ology: The art and science of creating great presentations.* O'Reilly Media, Inc.

Hutchinson, K. (2017). *A short primer on innovative evaluation*

reporting. Community Solutions Planning & Evaluation.

Medina, J. (2014). *Brain rules.* Pear Press.

Norman, D. A. (2004). *Emotional design: Why we love (or hate) everyday things.* Basic Books.

Smiciklas, M. (2012). *The power of infographics: Using pictures to communicate and connect with your audiences.* Que Publishing.

Torres, R. T., Preskill, H., & Piontek, M. E. (2005). *Evaluation strategies for communicating and reporting: Enhancing learning in organizations* (2nd ed.). SAGE.

Wilkerson, S. B., & Haden, C. M. (2014). Effective practices for evaluating STEM out-of-school time programs. *Afterschool Matters, 19*(1), 1019.

CHAPTER 2

Dunlap, J., & Lowenthal, R. (2016). Getting graphic about infographics: Design lessons learned from popular infographics. *Journal of Visual Literacy, 35*(1), 42–59. https://doi.org/10.1080/1051144X.2016.1205832

Gilliam, A., Davis, D., Barrington, T., Lacson, R., Uhl, G., & Phoenix, U. (2002). The value of engaging stakeholders in planning and implementing evaluations. *AIDS Education and Prevention: Official Publication of the International Society for AIDS Education, 14*(3 Suppl A), 5–17.

Haden, C., & Peery, E. (2021). *Evaluation of the NASA-Funded*

Planetary Learning that Advances the Nexus of Engineering, Technology, and Science (PLANETS) Project: Five-Year Summative Evaluation Report.

Smiciklas, M. (2012). *The power of infographics: Using pictures to communicate and connect with your audiences.* Que Publishing.

Yarbrough, D. B., Shulha, L. M., Hopson, R. K., & Caruthers, F. A. (2010). *The program evaluation standards: A guide for evaluators and evaluation users.* SAGE.

CHAPTER 3

Beegel, J. (2014). *Infographics for dummies.* John Wiley & Sons.

Cairo, A. (2016). *The truthful art: Data, charts, and maps for communication.* New Riders.

Creative Commons. (2021, August 28). *Frequently asked questions.* https://creativecommons.org/faq/

Duarte, N. (2010). *Resonate: Present visual stories that transform audiences.* Wiley & Sons, Inc.

Grant, M. (2013). What makes a good title? *Health Information & Libraries Journal, 30,* 259–260. https://doi.org/10.1111/hir.12049

Knaflic, C. (2015). *Storytelling with data: A data visualization guide for business professionals.* John Wiley and Sons.

Krum, R. (2014). *Cool infographics: Effective communication with data visualization and design.* John Wiley & Sons.

McGaugh, J. L. (2013). Making lasting memories: Remembering the significant. *Proceedings of the National Academy of Sciences, 110*(Supple2), 10402–10407. www.ncbi.nlm.nih.gov/pmc/articles/PMC3690616/

Nielsen, J. (2018). *How little do users read? Nielsen Norman Group.* https://www.nngroup.com/articles/how-little-do-users-read/

Paiva, C. E., da Silveira Nogueira Lima, J. P., & Paiva, B. S. R. (2012). Articles with short titles describing the results are cited more often. *Clinics, 67*(5), 509–513.

Paivio, A. (1971). Imagery and language. In S. Segal (Ed.), *Imagery* (pp. 7–32). Academic Press.

Subotic, S., & Mukherjee, B. (2014). Short and amusing: The relationship between title characteristics, downloads, and citations in psychology articles. *Journal of Information Science, 40*(1), 115–124.

University of Minnesota. (n.d.). *Writing an effective title.* Retrieved from http://writing.umn.edu/sws/assets/pdf/quicktips/titles.pdf

Weinreich, H., Obendorf, H., Herder, E., & Mayer, M. (2008). Not quite the average: An empirical study of Web use. *ACM Transactions on the Web (TWEB), 2*(1), 1–31.

wikiHow. (2021, February 3). *How to create a good story title.* https://www.wikihow.com/Create-a-Good-Story-Title

CHAPTER 4

Atchison, D. A., & Smith, G. (2000). Chapter 1 - The human eye: An overview. In D. A. Atchison & G. Smith (Eds.), *Optics of the human eye* (pp. 3–10). Butterworth-Heinemann.

Burgio, V., & Moretti, M. (2017). Infographics as images: Meaningfulness beyond information. *Multidisciplinary Digital Publishing Institute Proceedings, 1*(9), 891.

Cairo, A. (2016). *The truthful art: Data, charts, and maps for communication.* New Riders.

Creative Commons. (2021, August 28). *Frequently asked questions.* https://creativecommons.org/faq/

Devine, P. G. (1989). Stereotypes and prejudice: Their automatic and controlled components. *Journal of Personality and Social Psychology, 56*, 5–18.

Djamasbi, S., Siegel, M., & Tullis, T. (2010). Generation Y, web design, and eye tracking. *International Journal of Human-Computer Studies, 68*(5), 307–323.

Dunlap, J. C., & Lowenthal, P. R. (2016). Getting graphic about infographics: Design lessons learned from popular infographics. *Journal of Visual Literacy, 35*(1), 42–59.

Evergreen, S. (2017). *Effective data visualization: The right chart for the right data.* SAGE.

Evergreen, S. (2018). *Presenting data effectively: Communicating findings for maximum impact* (2nd ed.). SAGE.

Faraday, P. (2000). Visually critiquing web pages. In N. Correia, T. Chambel, & G. Davenport (Eds.), *Multimedia'99* (pp. 155–166). Springer.

Kirk, A. (2019). *Data visualisation: A handbook for data driven design* (2nd ed.). SAGE.

Knaflic, C. N. (2015). *Storytelling with data: A data visualization guide for business professionals.* Wiley.

Krum, R. (2014). *Cool infographics: Effective communication with data visualization and design.* John Wiley & Sons.

Medina, J. (2014). *Brain rules.* Pear Press.

Naidoo, R., Smith, B., Foster, C., & Chetty, V. (2022). Physical activity for adults with disabilities: Designing a South African infographic to communicate guidelines. *British Journal of Sports Medicine, 56*(10), 537–538. https://doi.org/10.1136/bjsports-2021-104855

Pickens, J. (1982). *Without bias: A guidebook for non-discriminatory communication* (2nd ed.). Inernational Association of Business Commmunicators.

Solso, R. L. (2003). *The psychology of art and the evolution of the conscious brain.* The MIT Press.

St. Amant, K. (2015). Culture and the contextualization of care: A prototype-based approach to developing health and medical visuals for international audiences.

Communication Design Quarterly Review, 3(2), 38–47.

Veletsianos, G. (2010). Contextually relevant pedagogical agents: Visual appearance, stereotypes, and first impressions and their impact on learning. *Computers & Education, 55*(2), 576–585.

Zikmund-Fisher, B. J., Witteman, H. O., Dickson, M., Fuhrel-Forbis, A., Kahn, V. C., Exe, N. L., Valerio, M., Holtzman, L. G., Scherer, L. D., & Fagerlin, A. (2014). Blocks, ovals, or people? Icon type affects risk perceptions and recall of pictographs. *Medical Decision Making: An International Journal of the Society for Medical Decision Making, 34*(4), 443–453. https://doi.org/10.11 77/0272989X13511706

Zull, J. E. (2002). *The art of changing the brain.* Stylus.

CHAPTER 5

Beegel, J. (2014). *Infographics for dummies.* John Willey & Sons, Inc.

Boulton, M. (2007). *Whitespace.* https://alistapart.com/article/whitespace

Clinton, V. (2019). Reading from paper compared to screens: A systematic review and meta-analysis. *Journal of Research in Reading, 42*(2), 288–325.

Fessenden, T. (2018). *Scrolling and attention.* Nielsen Norman Group. https://www.nngroup.com/articles/scrolling-and-attention/

Greussing, E., & Boomgaarden, H. G. (2021).

Promises and pitfalls: Taking a closer look at how interactive infographics affect learning from news. *International Journal of Communication* [Online], 3336+. https://link.gale.com/apps/doc/A679119454/AONE?u=googlescholar&sid=googleScholar&xid=60b8a7da

Krum, R. (2014). *Cool infographics: Effective communication with data visualization and design.* John Wiley & Sons.

Malamed, C. (2009). *Visual language for designers: Principles for creating graphics that people understand.* Rockport Publishers, Inc.

McCready, R. (2017). *How to pick the right infographic size for your blog post.* Venngage. https://venngage.com/blog/infographic-size/

O'Neill, K. (2016). *Pixels and place: Connecting human experience across physical and digital spaces.* KO Insights.

Sanchez, C. A., & Wiley, J. (2009). To scroll or not to scroll: Scrolling, working memory capacity, and comprehending complex texts. *Human Factors, 51*(5), 730–738. https://doi.org/10.1177/0018720809352788

Sharief, K. (2020). *What is a pixel? Definition, uses, features, and more.* Computer Tech Reviews. Retrieved September 5, 2022, from https://www.computertechreviews.com/definition/pixel/

Techopedia. (2020, August 31). *What is a pixel?* Techopedia.com. Retrieved September 4, 2022, from https://www.techopedia.com/definition/24012/pixel

Tversky, B. (2005). Functional significance of visuospatial representations. In P. Shah & A. Miyake (Eds.), *The Cambridge handbook of visuospatial thinking* (pp. 1–34). Cambridge University Press. https://doi.org/10.1017/CBO9780511610448.002

CHAPTER 6

Anderson, D., & Bowman, J. (2018, May 16). *Why so many Fast Food Logos are Red.* Business Insider. Retrieved July 14, 2022, from https://www.businessinsider.com/mcdonalds-wendys-burger-king-arbys-jack-in-the-box-red-logos-2018-5

Aslam, M. M. (2006). Are you selling the right colour? A cross-cultural review of colour as a marketing cue. *Journal of Marketing Communications, 12*(1), 15–30. https://doi.org/10.1080/13527260500247827

Babich, N. (2021, December 8). *6 simple tips on using color in your design - UX Planet.* Medium. https://uxplanet.org/5-simple-tips-on-using-color-in-your-design-40916d0dfa63

Ballast, D. K. (2002). *Interior design reference manual.* Professional Pub. Inc.

Bartram, L., Patra, A., & Stone, M. (2017). Affective color in visualization. In *Proceedings of the 2017 CHI Conference on Human Factors in Computing Systems (CHI '17).* Association for Computing Machinery, , 1364–1374. https://doi.org/10.1145/3025453.3026041

Brumberger, E. R. (2003). The rhetoric of typography: The persona of typeface and text. *Technical Communication, 50*(2), 206–223.

Cyr, D. (2008). Modeling web site design across cultures: Relationships to trust, satisfaction, and e-loyalty. *Journal of Management Information Systems, 24*(4), 47–72.

Djamasbi, S., Siegel, M., Tullis, T., & Dai, R. (2010, January). Efficiency, trust, and visual appeal: Usability testing through eye tracking. In *2010 43rd Hawaii International Conference on System Sciences* (pp. 1–10). IEEE.

Dzulkifli, M. A., & Mustafar, M. F. (2013). The influence of colour on memory performance: A review. *The Malaysian Journal of Medical Sciences: MJMS, 20*(2), 3.

Elliot, A. J. (2015). Color and psychological functioning: A review of theoretical and empirical work. *Frontiers in Psychology, 6*, 368.

Faraday, P. (2000). Visually critiquing web pages. In N. Correia, T. Chambel, & G. Davenport (Eds.), *Multimedia'99* (pp. 155–166). Springer.

Hemphill, M. (1996). A note on adults' color–emotion associations. *The Journal of Genetic Psychology, 157*(3), 275–280.

Jonauskaite, D., Wicker, J., Mohr, C., Dael, N., Havelka, J., Papadatou-Pastou, M., Zhang, M., & Oberfeld, D. (2019). A machine learning approach to quantify the specificity of colour–emotion associations and their cultural differences. *Royal Society Open Science, 6*,

190741. https://doi.org/10.1098/rsos.190741

Juni, S., & Gross, J. S. (2008). Emotional and persuasive perception of fonts. *Perceptual and Motor Skills, 106*, 35–42.

Knight, C., & Glaser, J. (2012, June 5). *Why subtle typographic choices make all the difference*. Smashing Magazine. Retrieved July 22, 2022, from https://www.smashingmagazine.com/2012/06/subtle-typographic-choices-make-difference/

Kuhbandner, C., Spitzer, B., Lichtenfeld, S., & Pekrun, R. (2015). Differential binding of colors to objects in memory: Red and yellow stick better than blue and green. *Frontiers in Psychology, 6*, 231.

Kulahcioglu, T., & de Melo, G. (2020, October). Fonts like this but happier: A new way to discover fonts. In *Proceedings of the 28th ACM International Conference on Multimedia* (pp. 2973–2981). Association for Computing Machinery.

Liu, J. (2010). *Color blindness & web design*. Usability.gov. Retrieved May 26, 2022, from https://www.usability.gov/get-involved/blog/2010/02/color-blindness.html

Malamed, C. (2009). *Visual language for designers: Principles for creating graphics that people understand*. Rockport Publishers, Inc.

Mukherjee, K., Yin, B., Sherman, B. E., Lessard, L., & Schloss, K. B. (2022). Context matters: A theory of semantic discriminability for perceptual encoding systems. *IEEE Transactions on Visualization and Computer Graphics, 28*(1), 697–706.

National Symbols. Ghana High Commission. (n.d.). Retrieved July 14, 2022, from https://ghanahighcom.org.au/site/flag-and-coat-of-arms

Naz, K. A. Y. A., & Helen, H. (2004). Color-emotion associations: Past experience and personal preference. In *AIC 2004 Color and Paints, Interim Meeting of the International Color Association, Proceedings* (Vol. 5, p. 31). Jose Luis Caivano.

Palmer, S. E., & Schloss, K. B. (2011). Ecological valence and theories of human color preference. In C. P. Biggam, C. Hough, D. Simmons, & C. Kay (Eds.), *New directions in colour studies*. John Benjamins.

Richardson, R. T., Drexler, T. L., & Delparte, D. M. (2014). Color and contrast in E-Learning design: A review of the literature and recommendations for instructional designers and web developers. *MERLOT Journal of Online Learning and Teaching, 10*(4), 657–670.

Schloss, K. B., Lessard, L., Walmsley, C. S., & Foley, K. (2018). Color inference in visual communication: The meaning of colors in recycling. *Cognitive Research: Principles and Implications, 3*, 5. https://doi.org/10.1186/s41235-018-0090-y

Singh, S. (2006). Impact of color on marketing. *Management Decision, 44*(6), 783–789. https://doi.org/10.1108/00251740610673332

Song, H., & Schwarz, N. (2008). If it's hard to read, it's hard to do: Processing fluency affects effort prediction and motivation. *Psychological Science, 19*,

986–988. doi:10.1111/j.1467-92 80.2009.02267

Spence, I., Wong, P., Rusan, M., & Rastegar, N. (2006). How color enhances visual memory for natural scenes. *Psychological Science, 17*(1), 1–6.

Sundar, A., Gonsales, F., & Schafer, G. (2018). Synchronicity in signage promotes a sense of belonging. *Interdisciplinary Journal of Signage and Wayfinding, 2*(2), 30–40.

WebFX. (2022, April 25). *Psychology of color: Infographic: Visual meaning.* Retrieved July 14, 2022, from https://www.webfx.com/blog/web-design/psychology-of-color-infographic/

Web Accessibility Initiative (WAI). (2022). *WCAG 2 overview.* Retrieved May 26, 2022, from https://www.w3.org/WAI/standards-guidelines/wcag/

CHAPTER 7

Coates, S. (2014). *White space: An overlooked element of design.* Honors College Capstone Experience/Thesis Projects. Paper 442. http://digitalcommons.wku.edu/stu_hon_theses/442

CHAPTER 8

GSA. (2019, December). *How to author and test Microsoft PowerPoint Presentations for accessibility. Section508.gov.* Retrieved July 14, 2022, from https://www.section508.gov/create/presentations/training-videos/

GSA. (2022, June 29). *IT Accessibility/Section 508.* Retrieved July 14, 2022, from https://www.gsa.gov/node/86686?gsaredirect=

Institute for Disability Research, Policy, and Practice. (2021, October 19). *Alternative text. WebAIM.* Retrieved July 14, 2022, from https://webaim.org/techniques/alttext/

Penn State Accessibility. (2018, September 17). *Accessibility checker for Microsoft Office.* Accessibility Checker for Microsoft Office. Retrieved July 14, 2022, from https://accessibility.psu.edu/microsoftoffice/checker/

CHAPTER 9

Djamasbi, S., Siegel, M., Tullis, T., & Dai, R. (2010, January). Efficiency, trust, and visual appeal: Usability testing through eye tracking. In *2010 43rd Hawaii international conference on system sciences* (pp. 1–10). IEEE.

Dunlap, J. C., & Lowenthal, P. R. (2016). Getting graphic about infographics: Design lessons learned from popular infographics. *Journal of Visual Literacy, 35*(1), 42–59.

Fessenden, T. (2018). *Scrolling and attention.* Nielsen Norman Group. https://www.nngroup.com/articles/scrolling-and-attention/

Grant, M. (2013). What makes a good title? *Health Information & Libraries Journal, 30*, 259–260. https://doi.org/10.1111/hir.12049

Kirk, A. (2016). *Data visualisation: A handbook for data driven design* (2nd ed.). SAGE.

Knaflic, C. (2015). *Storytelling with data: A data visualization guide for business professionals.* John Wiley and Sons.

Knight, C., & Glaser, J. (2012, June 5). *Why subtle typographic choices make all the difference. Smashing Magazine.* Retrieved July 22, 2022, from https://www.smashingmagazine.com/2012/06/subtle-typographic-choices-make-difference/

Krum, R. (2014). *Cool infographics: Effective communication with data visualization and design.* John Wiley & Sons.

Kulahcioglu, T., & de Melo, G. (2020, October). Fonts like this but happier: A new way to discover fonts. In *Proceedings of the 28th ACM International Conference on Multimedia* (pp. 2973–2981). Association for Computing Machinery.

Medina, J. (2008). *Brain rules: 12 principles for surviving and thriving at work, home, and school.* Pear Press.

Nielsen, J. (2018). *How little do users read? Nielsen Norman Group.* https://www.nngroup.com/articles/how-little-do-users-read/

Palmer, S. E., & Schloss, K. B. (2011). Ecological valence and theories of human color preference. In C. P. Biggam, C. Hough, D. Simmons, & C. Kay (Eds.), *New directions in colour studies.* John Benjamins.

Subotic, S., & Mukherjee, B. (2014). Short and amusing: The relationship between title characteristics, downloads, and citations in psychology articles. *Journal of Information Science, 40*(1), 115–124.

Weinreich, H., Obendorf, H., Herder, E., & Mayer, M. (2008). Not quite the average: An empirical study of Web use. *ACM Transactions on the Web (TWEB), 2*(1), 1–31.

Zikmund-Fisher, B. J., Witteman, H. O., Dickson, M., Fuhrel-Forbis, A., Kahn, V. C., Exe, N. L., Valerio, M., Holtzman, L. G., Scherer, L. D., & Fagerlin, A. (2014). Blocks, ovals, or people? Icon type affects risk perceptions and recall of pictographs. *Medical Decision Making, 34*(4), 443–453. https://doi.org/10.1177/02 72989X13511706

CHAPTER 10

Krum, R. (2014). *Cool infographics: Effective communication with data visualization and design.* John Wiley & Sons.

Smiciklas, M. (2012). *The power of infographics: Using pictures to communicate and connect with your audiences.* Que Publishing.

INDEX